PUFI

*Editoi*

PON



The world is full of books about ponies, written for children. This is completely different – a book about children, written for ponies. Instead of the child teaching the pony how to jump – as if it didn't *know* – it is the pony who teaches the child how to ride.

From a pony's point of view all riding schools have the same thing wrong with them: they are for children who *can't* ride. As soon as a child becomes bearable, she vanishes and has a pony of her own, and her place is taken by another. The newcomers are certain to scream when the pony walks and as likely to fall off as soon as it comes to a halt. 'Here we go again!' the ponies grumble, and who can blame them?

No wonder that the eight ponies at Daisy Dedleigh-Skirett's Riding School decided to change things. Prune, for instance, decided to try bucking the new pupils off at the very beginning. 'If I did that,' he argued, 'Daisy would get rid of me and I should have a little girl of my own.' (All ponies realize that a little girl is something designed by nature to look after a pony.) So Prune tried it, but it did no good.

Old Smokey, who knew all the answers, told them, 'It is not enough to be unwanted *here*. You have first to find the girl you want and a home you would prefer.' So under his tuition the ponies each decided what sort of girl they would like, and how they were to train and discipline her when they had her. Then Daisy announced her engagement. This meant that she would give up the Riding School. It also meant that the ponies would really have new homes, and have to put into practice all that Smokey had taught them about a pony's secret weapons – the head, the teeth, the hooves and the whinny. And if you don't want to know what happens after reading this, then you just don't like ponies.

C. NORTHCOTE PARKINSON

# PONIES PLOT

*Illustrated by Violet Morgan*

PUFFIN BOOKS

Puffin Books, Penguin Books Ltd,
Harmondsworth, Middlesex, England
Penguin Books Australia Ltd, Ringwood, Victoria, Australia
Penguin Books (N.Z.) Ltd,
182–190 Wairau Road, Auckland 10, New Zealand

—

First published by John Murray 1965
Published in Penguin Books 1968
Reprinted 1970, 1972, 1973, 1974


—

Made and printed in Great Britain by
Cox & Wyman Ltd, London, Reading and Fakenham
Set in Monotype Imprint

TO SPICE

# CONTENTS


| | | |
|---|---|---|
| | Preface | 9 |
| 1 | Miss Lawkinson's Pa | 13 |
| 2 | The Eight Ponies | 27 |
| 3 | Dismounted Rally | 40 |
| 4 | The Pony Club Camp | 53 |
| 5 | Spice goes Hunting | 64 |
| 6 | Brighty's Christmas | 72 |
| 7 | The Pony Club Gymkhana | 82 |
| 8 | Spice goes on a Voyage | 95 |
| 9 | Astrohorse Prune | 106 |
| 10 | Spice on Parade | 115 |
| 11 | Space-age Pony | 125 |
| 12 | Smokey goes Home | 135 |

# PREFACE

THE world is full of books about ponies, written for children. This is completely different, a book about children, written for ponies. Such ponies as have studied the work in manuscript agree that there should be a copy in every loosebox. Why? Because the stories are told from the pony's point of view. That the pony *has* a point of view is only now being recognized. In the ordinary run of pony books the story centres on a small girl who dreams of ponies, wants a pony, secures a pony for nothing (saving it from ill-treatment in a gypsy encampment), rides it with growing confidence and ends with First Prize in the Hunter Trials. Among ponies, however, the same story would be told with the pony as hero. Ill-treated and underfed, Blackie dreams about children, wants a child for himself, plans to attract Brenda's attention, defeats the scheme of a rival pony, saves the girl from drowning, wins over the reluctant parents and finally (guess what?) wins First Prize in the Hunter Trials. The story may be similar but is told from the opposite point of view. Instead of the child teaching the pony how to jump – as if it didn't *know* – it is the pony who teaches the child how to ride. We need not ask which story is nearer the truth. It is enough to grasp that Ponies Plot.

The stories which follow were mostly told to me by my friends Fairy and Spice, to whom I am deeply indebted. But in a book for ponies the pictures are just as important as the text; even more so, perhaps, for ponies who cannot read. So we were very fortunate in persuading Violet Morgan to do the illustrations for us. Her likenesses of the eight ponies are excellent and rather flattering than otherwise. Only Prune objects to his portrait, but then he *would*. We can't hope to please every animal and even Smokey thought he should look a bit younger. I am lucky again in having publishers who like horses and realize that every stable should have its bookshelf. To them I must express my thanks, as also to Mrs Joan K. Neill, who typed the manuscript, and Miss Nancy Robin, who saved me from many interruptions.

To my younger daughter I owe the debt which every author must owe to his first critic. But while Charles, Antonia and Jonathan have added somewhat to my experience of the stable yard, no part of the book is based on any actual incident in their childhood. I should emphasize, indeed, that the human characters in the book are just as imaginary as the events, the Port Bygone Branch of the Pony Club bearing no resemblance to any actual Branch, and its officers being not only fictitious but highly improbable.

To Ann my thanks are more difficult to express. Without her there would have been no children, no ponies and no book. To her, in the ordinary way, the book should have been dedicated. But I had to remind myself that this book is meant for ponies, not for children and still less for parents. To a pony, therefore, the book is addressed. The choice lay between two of them,

Fairy and Spice; the first a Welsh blonde and the second a Dartmoor roan. Spice was chosen – it matters not by whom – but Fairy, who is on loan from a beloved grandmother, has been promised the heroine's part in the expected sequel. Privately, however, I hope she will forget about it, for 'A Book of Fairy Stories' would convey, as a title, the wrong idea.

C. NORTHCOTE PARKINSON

*Les Câches House*
*St Martin's*
GUERNSEY

I

# MISS LAWKINSON'S PA

IT is some years now since Miss Daisy Dedleigh-Sirkett kept the Dundreary Riding School at Dedford Ditchbury in Dorset. She is married now and lives twenty miles away at Bassett St Giles. At the time, however, when our story opens she had daily classes and constant confusion. It was in her father's paddock that half the members of the Pony Club learnt to ride, and it was there that many of their ponies learnt to be ridden. Daisy was then a frowning nineteen-year-old who spent part of each day sorting out the muddles she had made the day before; muddles about what was to happen and when. Her daily telephone conversations could be heard through the window at the back of the farmhouse, sounding rather like this:

'But I thought Susan was to be on the 9 o'clock ride – I have her down in the book for 9.0. . . . Well, I'll try to fit her in somehow, although we now have too many at 10.30. . . . What, is she really? Then why didn't Mrs Overwaite *tell* me that Deirdre would be coming at 9.0? Oh, well! See you at the Pony Club Rally on Saturday. . . . What's that? No! But they can't have changed the time *again*!! . . . At Larchington? But we had all *agreed* that it should be Nettlewood Common! . . . Very well, then. We'll see Susan at 10.15.' Daisy was popular, on the whole, with the girls and their mothers, but not with the boys, nor with the ponies.

Daisy's ponies numbered eight in all. Oldest of them was Old Smokey, aged about twenty and good for beginners. As quiet but impossibly lazy was Dunblane, a rather useless animal. Prune was a half-witted piebald, rather looked down upon by the better ponies, Mischief, Brighty and Spice. Best in the Show Ring was Skylark and the best show jumper (at that time) was Unbeatable. These ponies had, it is true, the advantage of each other's company. In all other ways they found the work boring and tiresome. Round and round the paddock they would go, with Daisy yelping, 'Now trot on, Mabel! Heels *down*, hands *low*!' On other days, being anxious not to overwork the ponies before a Rally, Daisy would keep them standing still while she went over the parts of the harness. Mischief found this so wearisome that he often tried to give his rider the answer. 'The throat lash, you nit!' he would try to mutter from the side of his mouth, but Kate (or Jenny, as the case might be) was never able to take the hint. It is the sad fact that horses, who can talk to each other, and to dogs, are almost dumb where human beings are concerned. An intelligent pony has lots to say but children, the little horrors, are never listening. In a Riding School, more especially, the pony's life can be very dull indeed. And for dullness Daisy's school was in a class by itself.

If some Riding Schools are worse than others, the others must presumably be better than some. But they are all open to one objection from the pony's point of view; they are all for the children who *can't* ride. As soon as Margaret begins to know her stuff, having learnt how to stay on when jumping, she disappears. If not

informed by rumour, Daisy's other pupils would gather what had happened from the telephone conversations they overheard.

'I'm so glad that Betty can come on Tuesday. . . . Oh, sorry, didn't you *say* Tuesday? . . . Yes, Thursday will do but can she come at 9.0? Oh, I see; you want her to be in the same ride as Margaret. . . . Yes, I *do* understand. . . . But I don't think Margaret will be here. . . . No, not on Tuesday either. . . . Nor on Wednesday. . . . The fact is, we are losing her. She is to have her own pony, arriving Monday. . . . Yes, quite absurd, of course! In another year or two, perhaps, she would – Oh, no, she didn't ask *my* advice! . . . Yes I do agree. . . . I think Betty's father is perfectly right. . . . Not until she is ready to take full responsibility. . . . Why *should* he have to muck out the stables – why indeed? I'll tell Betty myself that she needs a Lot More Instruction. . . . Very well then. On Thursday at nine.'

It was easy to guess that another pony had found a good home. 'And so it goes on!' the Riding School ponies would tell each other. Each child vanished at the very moment she had become tolerable, those with almost equine intelligence being the first to go. And the place of each would be taken by another five-year-old – one certain to scream when the pony walked and as likely to fall off as soon as it came to a halt. 'Here we go again!' the ponies would grumble, and who would blame them? Discussing things in the lower meadow, the ponies used to propose bucking the new pupils off at the outset.

'If I did that,' said Prune, 'Daisy would let me go and I should have a little girl of my own.' All ponies realize that a little girl is something designed by nature to look after a pony. But not every pony has a girl to himself, much as he would like to have one.

'Try it and see,' replied Old Smokey and that was what Prune did. Little Rosemary was removed howling and Prune had no more five-year-olds. It did him no good, however, as Daisy now thought him ideal for More Advanced Pupils: and especially for those, like Betty, who thought they knew it all.

'Yes,' she would coo on the telephone. 'On Friday then, the 13th. She can ride *Prune*. . . . *Vicious?* Oh, dear, no! But Betty should ride a more *lively* pony now. She has ridden Old Smokey quite long enough. It makes her just a little *too* confident, if you know what I mean. . . . See that she wears a hard hat. . . . No, we don't want her to start thinking of the Olympic Team! . . . Very well, then, on Friday.'

Bucking, clearly, got you nowhere. It was Mischief who next proposed a different scheme.

'What if I were to bite Daisy when there is nobody looking?'

'That's right!' said Prune eagerly. 'Take a large piece out of her jodhpurs just before a promising parent (mother of six) is due to pay her first visit!'

'Or else I could do something with the upper half of my stable door,' said Mischief thoughtfully. 'She sometimes leaves it unfastened and ajar. Now, if I put my head behind it, and waited . . .'

'Until you heard her footsteps on the concrete . . .'

'Exactly! Then I could give a quick shove . . .'

'And knock the silly girl for six!' concluded Prune, dancing with glee.

'Then Daisy would believe that I have some Minor Drawbacks, known to her but to nobody else. She would be only too keen to say "good-bye".'

'RUBBISH!' said Old Smokey and all the other ponies looked in his direction.

'Nonsense!' he went on, 'and likewise DRIVEL! You youngsters don't see what the problem is. It is not enough to be unwanted *here*. You have first to find the girl you want and a home you would prefer. You must learn to look ahead! Decide, first of all, what it is you want.'

'Well,' said Skylark, 'I should choose a girl of about nine, standing about fifteen hooves and weighing not more than four stone twelve pounds.'

'Or *less*,' said Dunblane quickly.

'She should have a snub nose,' said Brighty in a dreamy way, 'with fair or red hair – yes, and freckles – '

'Freckles, yes,' agreed Skylark. 'But a brunette can be all right, too, so long as her back is straight and her legs are long.'

'I actually *prefer* a brunette with straight hair,' said Spice. 'But she needs to be dependable, generous and kind, nicely mannered and reasonably intelligent.'

'Not too confident or rash,' suggested Dunblane.

'But with *at least* three years' experience,' said Unbeatable.

'All right!' grunted Smokey. 'Those are the Points we look for in the child. But what about her family and background?'

'She should have a prosperous father,' Unbeatable replied, 'a doting mother – both ready to help out in the stables. Yes, and two younger sisters aged five and one.'

'And what about brothers?'

'Only one, I think,' said Unbeatable. 'Well-behaved and useful with apples.'

'Correct!' admitted the oldest pony. 'Now what about the home itself?'

'It should have a range of looseboxes,' answered Skylark, 'with good forage space and room for friends; a sheltered paddock, a good meadow with running water, trees to give shade in summer. . . . Yes, I think that is all.'

'Ah!' said Old Smokey, 'you have all forgotten one thing. The ideal family should also have a habit of keeping animals for ever, even when old, yes, and feeble.'

'Quite so,' said Mischief. 'We younger ones were not looking so far ahead.'

'Too true you weren't,' muttered Old Smokey. 'But now you should begin to see the difficulty. The ideal girl – the one with all the advantages we have agreed upon – is None Too Common. And what we want is just what every other pony wants. So the best stables are not vacant for long!'

'How right you are!' sighed Brighty. 'And all the mothers want the same sort of pony – about twelve hands, quiet and sensible but not lazy, attractive to look at but able to jump, well-schooled but young, safe but willing. The fact is, we are not all ideal enough for the ideal girl, even if we could find her. And some of us are – well – not ideal at all!'

There was some bickering after this, Dunblane asking

why Brighty should have looked at *him* while making that last remark. Prune said that some ponies were a great deal too quiet and Mischief had a theory that schooling could be carried too far. Unbeatable suggested, rather cheekily, that Old Smokey might himself find it difficult to secure the ideal home, being no longer quite the pony he had been. The others all looked at him, wondering whether he would take offence. But Smokey merely chuckled.

'You think I am too old?' he said. 'Well, maybe I am. And some of you may be thinking that I was no Derby winner at the best of times, and maybe you could be right. But I had the ideal home once, long ago, for all that. Would you young ponies like to hear about it?' They all agreed politely that they would, and gathered round to hear another chapter of Smokey's life history. He was well known for his stories of the good old days when Horses were Horses. They had helped to pass many a dull hour in the stable yard.

'When I was younger than any of you, little more than a foal, I lived at the Livery Stable at Liversedge. I was called Soot in those days, my coat being the same sort of colour as now but maybe a little darker.'

'A sort of dirty grey?' suggested the intolerable Prune.

'A well-chosen dark shade, restrained and neat,' snapped Smokey. 'Not one of those patchy jobs, now this and now that, neither here nor there!' The other ponies sniggered and Prune hung his head in piebald confusion. 'But my life at the Livery Stables was sheer misery.'

'Why was that, Smokey?' asked Spice.

'Well, the Proprietor was liverish and all the other animals much larger than I was. Life among those wretched hacks was dreary, neigh, *impossible.* I often planned to run away – dreamt of the New Forest and a life of freedom.'

'But you never risked it?' asked Brighty.

'No, I remembered in time that I am not a New Forest Pony. I came originally from Wales, actually, and that was a long train-journey away and I with no ticket. Could I have bluffed the railwaymen or travelled under the seat? I decided – and I think wisely – that it could not be done. One day, however, a wonderful little girl looked over my stable door and called out 'Look, Pa – isn't he simply adorable?'

'She called out – *what*?' asked Unbeatable.

'You heard,' replied Smokey with a touch of annoyance. 'I was younger then. Well, this girl was called Lorna. She was just right for age, looks, size and everything. A girl in a thousand with apple peelings by the handful. Her father, who presently joined her at the stable door, looked countrified and prosperous. His name (I learnt afterwards) was Lawkinson. Wealthy? He was rolling in the stuff. He was the sort of man to whom lump sugar meant literally nothing – he could have lived on it if he had liked. I could see at a glance that he would have acres of grass and stacks of hay. As for Lorna and me, it was a case, on both sides, of love at first sight. But Lorna's Pa gave me hardly so much as a glance. Instead of admiring me – as anyone might – he was looking round the loosebox. Having studied it carefully from back to front and from side to side he groaned with all the sadness that a groan can well express. "Muck," he sighed, "spreads so as to cover the stable floor available." '

'Good grief!' exclaimed Spice, looking thoroughly bewildered. 'What did he expect? I mean, what else can muck do?'

'I shouldn't have thought that a very *nice* subject to discuss,' said Skylark, and all the other ponies agreed that Mr Lawkinson's attitude was utterly absurd.

'Absurd or not,' said Smokey firmly, 'what he said was perfectly true. There was muck simply everywhere in that loosebox, not a clean patch of straw to be seen. Not that it made any difference to Lorna, mind you. She said at once that it didn't matter. "I shall do the mucking out," she pleaded, "and think what it will do for the strawberries!" There was a pause and she added, rather hastily, "I mean, for the *roses*!"

' "You say that, Lorna, but I know better," replied her father, "we had this arrangement before, the time you wanted a spaniel puppy. Remember? You were to feed it and exercise it and look after it. But who does the work? I do! What's more, I did all the work from the day it came!"

' "Yes, Pa, but I was young then. I am eight now and that makes all the difference. I shall call him Thundercloud!" '

'And did she?' asked Skylark.

'She did no such thing,' snapped Smokey. 'There has been confusion enough about my name as it is. And she turned down her father's idea of calling me Thunderbox. But her pleading was hard to resist. She had never (she said) wanted anything so much. Couldn't she have what she wanted, just this once?'

'I'll bet she had *always* had what she wanted,' was Mischief's comment.

'Of course she had!' was Smokey's reply. 'But her father stood firm on this occasion. He just said "No!" and stuck to it.'

'How terrible!' sighed Brighty.

'Terrible it was,' said Smokey, 'and worse than you know. For I made a few casual inquiries afterwards and learnt that Lorna was all and more than I had dared imagine. Her Pa had the most beautiful stables for miles around, with a white-fenced paddock and a huntsman weather-vane on the coach house gable. His garden was famous for roses and everyone agreed that he would do still better at the Horticultural Show if only he had some Organic Manure on the spot. Having learnt all this, I came to make a great decision . . .'

'And what was that?' asked Spice.

'I decided on a policy.'

'But *what* policy?' asked Mischief.

'A consistent policy. Something you would none of you have imagined.'

'I know, Smokey!' said Unbeatable. 'I have guessed it. You always used the same corner of the loosebox!'

'Exactly,' said Smokey, rather put out (for he had wanted to keep them guessing). 'Yes, that *was* my plan. But not the whole of it, mind you. Not by any means. I had still to bring Influence to bear upon the Proprietor of the Livery Stables.'

'I know, I know!' said Mischief excitedly. 'Your stable door, top half, had been left unfastened and ajar. So you chose your moment –'

'All right, you win,' replied Smokey rather crossly. 'It was something on those lines. By next day the Proprietor had a black eye and a pony to spare. And when Miss Lawkinson's Pa came round again, he was shown my loosebox, with just the one corner used and all the rest of the straw both clean and dry. He scarcely bothered to argue about the money, being eager to say 'Done!' before the Livery Stables man could change his mind. So I went home with Lorna. They were good years after that, those I spent at Borough Farm. I never had so good a home again.'

'But why did you ever leave?' asked Spice. 'Why aren't you there now? What happened?'

'*Lorna grew up*,' said Smokey briefly. 'Don't you realize that our good times always end like that? Children get bigger and the time comes when they give up riding; or, if they ride, they want a larger pony and then, later, a horse. The old pony has to go, and Lorna, you see, had no younger sister or brother. She must be married by now and maybe has children of her own. I shan't see Lorna again, nor the like of her. But I told you this story for a reason. Brighty said just now that we couldn't all have the ideal stable because we are not all of us the ideal pony. He was right, goodness knows! But what all you young ponies should remember is this; you can all be ideal in *one* way if only you put your minds to it!'

You might expect to hear, after this, that all seven of

them were reformed characters from that hour, always using the same corner of the loosebox. But that would not be true. They had all forgotten Old Smokey's advice in a day or two and Smokey himself was no better than the rest. All that the others could remember was that Smokey long ago had had a wonderful girl called Lorna and that he could never expect to see her again.

And were the ponies sad to think that even the best home (could they find it) would not last for ever? Not they! The present was enough for them and they presently heard some very exciting news. Rumour had it that Daisy was engaged to be married! It turned out, moreover, to be true. Her engagement was to be for a year, her wedding the following spring. This meant that she would give up the Riding School. It also meant that her ponies would each have to find a new home. Fond of her they had never been but they now agreed in wishing her well. They even talked of subscribing to give her a wedding present. Their minds were much more, however, on their own fortunes. A few felt confident of going to live with children they already knew, pupils of Daisy or members of the Pony Club. Others had no idea what the future had to offer them. 'Not another Riding School!' they all agreed; and there was, in fact, nobody eager to take Daisy's place at Dedford Ditchbury. So all the pony's talk that spring was of the wonderful homes they hoped to have. Whatever happened, each of them promised to keep in touch with the rest. They would meet, or at least hear news of each other through the Club. It was all very exciting for the younger ones but Old Smokey looked rather sad. Who would want an old pony like him? Whoever it was, the good old days had gone for good. There would never be another girl like Lorna.

## 2

# THE EIGHT PONIES

MILES away from Dorset and far from Dedford Ditchbury there lived a little girl called Jennifer. Her home was at Blackheath, where you might expect to meet highwaymen riding over dark moorlands under a threatening sky. But Blackheath is not really like that, nor is it ideal for riding at all. It is part of London, with houses stretching in all directions, and the heath (although a useful space for playing games or flying a kite) has a stream of traffic on every side. Jennifer's father was a scientist and said to be terribly clever. When asked what he did, Jennifer would say that his work had to do with rockets and space and all that sort of thing. When further questions followed, Jennifer would admit that he had never actually been to the moon – not as far as Jennifer knew – and that he didn't even talk of going there. He was more concerned, she thought, with designing the sort of rocket that would reach Mars or Venus. 'Daddy,' she would conclude proudly, 'is a physicist.' It was a difficult word to say and she was not at all sure what it meant, but people used to nod vaguely and say, 'How interesting!' before they went on to talk of something else.

Jennifer had her first experience of riding while on holiday near Tunbridge Wells. She had dreamed of ponies ever since, asking her parents why she couldn't keep a pony and ride before breakfast on the heath and in

Greenwich Park. There were, she was told, many difficulties about this, beginning with a lack of stabling in their second-floor flat and ending with the traffic problems of New Cross and the Romney Road. She would not ride again, it was clear, until next summer; and there was talk, even then, about going to the Norfolk Broads. In the meanwhile, Jennifer took the dog (a poodle called Snuff) for walks across the heath, usually preferring the Greenwich side from which she could glimpse, sometimes, the dome of St Paul's, with high ground beyond which might be Hampstead Heath. Whenever she hurried, her imaginary pony was trotting, and whenever she ran her pony was doing a canter or gallop. She was careful, however, in crossing the road and Snuff had learnt that he had to be careful too.

One day Jennifer varied her usual walk by going in quite the opposite direction. She wandered into an area which she had seldom visited and there came across what seemed to her the most wonderful shop she had ever seen. It was called 'The Oriental Store' and the window was filled with brocade and ivory, coloured lanterns and gaily painted toys. Even Snuff thought that the place had an interesting smell, and Jennifer could not drag herself away. What fixed her attention, however, was a picture. Or was it a picture? It was the wrong shape, to begin with, as compared with other pictures she had seen. It was long and narrow, unframed, and hung from the top by a length of tape. In this tall space the artist had drawn and coloured a landscape with funny twisted trees, misty mountains at the back and a river near the front. Dotted round this landscape were ponies, no two of them alike. Making a careful count of them, counting again to make sure, Jennifer concluded that there were eight ponies in all, and not a single human being. And each pony was doing something different. One was standing still, another was cantering briskly, a third was prancing with its forefeet off the ground and a fourth was rolling on its back. Jennifer stood, entranced, wondering from what land this exciting picture had come. Later, when she told her father about it, he said, 'That sounds like a Chinese scroll.' He was right, as fathers often are, but not very interested. His preference, unfortunately, was for boats.

Jennifer's walks with Snuff now took her repeatedly past the Oriental Store windows. Each time she gazed at the ponies and each time she feared that they would be gone before she could return. Grown-ups, after all, must come that way, each with a whole pocketful of money; and who, seeing that picture, and having the money, could possibly resist buying it? She admitted to herself that a picture is useful only up to a point. You can look at it and you can make up stories about it, guessing what had happened just before and what would happen after the moment which the picture represents. It never occurred to Jennifer, however, to go into the shop and ask what price they wanted. For most of her pocket money was spent on Snuff, leaving her with no more than ninepence for herself. She knew, however, that her eighth birthday would happen in three weeks' time (on March 8th) and that her Aunt Violet, who lived in Lewisham, might give her five shillings. With a full purse, she might enter the shop bravely. In the meanwhile she gazed and dreamed and worried whenever anyone else showed an interest in Oriental Art. To any other window-shopper she wanted to say, 'Don't waste time on this stuff. It's all faked – made in Birmingham, most likely – and dreadfully expensive!' But she couldn't say that out loud. Nor would it have made much sense, coming from a girl who didn't even know what the prices were.

On perhaps her fourth or fifth visit it seemed to her, for a moment, that the worst was about to happen. Two elderly gentlemen had paused outside the Oriental Store and were looking over the goods displayed. Worse still, they were discussing the very scroll which she had come to regard as hers!

'Not bad,' said the one in the heavy duffle coat. 'Modern, of course, probably painted in Hong-Kong or Penang. But a nice picture for all that.'

'Why are you so sure that it is modern?' asked the one who wore the monocle. 'I should have thought it quite antique – T'ang, you know, or Sung; or possibly Ming!'

'The style would make you think so, but the ponies are not really Chinese. The artist has been influenced a bit by what he has seen at the racecourse.'

'I see what you mean, and yet the mountains and trees are pretty much what you see in the classic pictures.'

'Oh, yes – and the artist sticks to the story, with *eight* ponies, no more, and no less.'

'What *is* the story, though?'

'Don't you know?' exclaimed the gentleman in the duffle coat. 'Well, it goes like this. A princess of long ago had eight ponies and was devoted to them. The time came for her to marry and her husband lived far away. She went to that distant country but had to leave her ponies behind.'

'Very sad for the poor girl!' murmured the gentleman with the monocle. 'I was pretty depressed myself when I had to leave my polo ponies in India.'

'Exactly. Well, years later, she came back on a visit to her parents, and when she came in sight, the ponies all knew her at once. They were terribly glad to see her but each one expressed his pleasure in a different way, one prancing, one rolling and so on. So in a Chinese picture of horses they usually number eight, and that is the story the picture is meant to illustrate.'

'That's very interesting. I never knew that before. Now you mention it, however, I can remember seeing that sort of picture in Singapore – or was it Malacca?'

'Ah, there used to be some good Chinese stuff in Malacca – in the old days, I mean. . . .'

The two elderly gentlemen walked on, still talking about the Old Days. Neither of them (to Jennifer's relief) seemed to want the picture, or indeed anything else in the shop. But now she knew the story and the scroll seemed all the more valuable. It remained to be seen whether Aunt Violet would remember Jennifer's birthday, as a good Aunt should.

When the day came Aunt Violet was even more generous than usual, sending Jennifer not five shillings but ten! With a fortune now to spend, Jennifer hurried that afternoon to the Oriental Store, scarcely believing that the scroll could be still in the window. Ten to one, she thought, some other retired Colonel would have buzzed up in a wheelchair, grabbed the picture and gone. But so far, at least, her fears were baseless. There was the scroll and there were the eight ponies, no more and no fewer. Now a person of wealth, to whom ninepence more or less meant literally nothing, Jennifer sailed into the shop like the important customer she was. The door tinkled when she closed it and the gust of wind which entered with her sent the lanterns swaying and the kimonos swinging. A little old man appeared from the back of the shop and peered at her through his spectacles.

'Good afternoon,' said Jennifer quickly, 'I'd like to buy the eight ponies in the window!' The little old man looked surprised at first but Jennifer explained that she was talking about the scroll.

'Oh, I see,' chuckled the old man. 'The Chinese painting on silk.' He brought it in from the window and allowed her to have a closer look at it. Whether old or not it was certainly very dirty. Close at hand, Jennifer liked it rather less, wondering how she could clean it.

'An interesting picture and very, very old. To you – well – I could let you have it for fifteen guineas.'

'But it isn't old!' Jennifer protested. 'Look at those ponies! Don't tell me that they are Tung – I mean Ham – or whatever it is. Nor Bing, either!'

The old man laughed until he had to rub his spectacles.

'All right!' he said. 'I'll let them go for ten pounds.'

As a bargainer, she had done pretty well, but it was all to no purpose. Ten pounds is much the same as fifteen guineas for someone whose purse contains exactly twelve shillings and fourpence-halfpenny.

'Oh, dear!' she said, on the verge of tears. 'I can't afford that much, and I did want those eight ponies – dirty as they are. I love them just like the princess did in the story.'

'So you know the story, do you?' said the shopkeeper. 'Perhaps you are more interested in ponies than in Chinese painting?'

'But of course! And those ponies are the ones I like best because each of them is doing something different!'

The old man chuckled again and came from behind the counter. Going over to the other side of the shop he opened a drawer and took out a cardboard box. From inside that he took a wooden box, about the size of one that might have contained chocolates. This he opened and removed the tissue paper, finally revealing eight ponies made of china, each fitting into a separate space of its own!

'In that case,' said the old shopkeeper, 'you might be interested in *these* ponies. . . .'

'But they are the same!' cried Jennifer. 'They are the ponies of the picture, and look – each one is different, just as in the story! But these are ever so much better. They are clean and I could move them around and play with them.' An awful thought then occurred to her. 'But I suppose,' she ended sadly, 'these will be even *more* expensive than the picture!' At this the old man chuckled afresh and showed her the price label, which read 10*s*. 'But for *you*,' he added, 'the price will be only

*7s. 6d.* How will that do? Shall I wrap them up for you?'

Half an hour later Jennifer was in her bedroom with the ponies arranged on the windowsill. She was trying to decide how to name them all. But her mother interrupted her with the news that the first guest had come rather early for her birthday tea-party. 'Bridget and Ruth have come, dear!' So they had, being accompanied by their mother, Mrs Nattering. 'Many happy returns, Jennifer!' said the twins and 'Many happy returns, dear!' said their mother.

The Natterings lived farther out of London and Jennifer had heard that they were going to have a pony. So she asked at once whether their pony had come. 'Of course!' laughed Mrs Nattering. 'I had forgotten what a keen horsewoman you became last summer! But we changed our plans a little and decided to have *two* ponies, one for each of the twins. You must come and see them some day. I don't suppose that you will be able to keep one here – so difficult, I mean, living in a flat – even as nice a flat as this with its view of the heath – there could be nowhere better for anyone who *has* to live in London, and I wouldn't mind it myself, not a bit; except, I mean, for the lack of space. But it is nice, I'll admit, to have open fields around and a paddock and stables. We have got the local carpenter to make us some jumps – cavaletti, I think they are called, such a *clever* idea, I always think, being able to use them in so many different ways. And the two ponies will be just right for the twins – we think of calling them Tweedledum and Tweedledee.'

Jennifer's mother thought that this twittering about ponies had gone on long enough. It was Jennifer's birthday, after all, and the child would be getting jealous. So like Mrs Nattering to go on like that!

'How lucky you are!' she said. 'And now Bridget and

Ruth must come and see Jennifer's new doll's house. Rather a nice one – it even has electric light!'

But Jennifer needed no reminder of how lucky *she* was in other ways. For she felt superior now even in the matter of ponies. As sweetly as possible she congratulated the twins on having their own animals to ride. Then she turned to their mother, congratulating her in turn on her paddock and cavaletti.

'How nice for you to have the *two* ponies,' she said, watching the lady's self-satisfied smile. The smile vanished, however, when she added – still more sweetly – 'I have EIGHT!'

Mrs Nattering left in rather a huff after that, saying that she would fetch the twins at six. From that point the party went well, with jelly, ice-cream and balloons. But when the games were over and when the last guest had gone, Jennifer's Daddy gave her the best present of all – better than anything she could have imagined. Making her sit on his knee, with Mummy beside them on the sofa, Daddy announced that he had been appointed to the Space Research Establishment at Newcombe Jettage!

'So that was the secret behind your trip to Dorset!' said Jennifer's mother. 'I thought you were being rather mysterious.'

'I didn't want to disappoint you, darling. The Director might have decided against having me. But now it is all settled and we shall be moving there almost immediately. Dr Glumley is leaving and we are to have his house at Windfall Orchard.'

Jennifer could hardly believe her ears. 'Shall we be in

the country?' she asked. 'With fields and woods all round?'

'Yes, Jennifer – in Dorset.'

'And is that near the sea?'

'Pretty near. Look, I'll show you where we shall be. Here is the map I used when I drove there last week. Here is Weymouth, here is Dorchester, here is Melbury and *there*, towards Bridport, is Newcombe Jettage. We are near the sea – Port Bygone would be the nearest seaside place – and there are some hills to the North – *here* – round Mickleby Moorside. I saw one other thing that would interest *you*, Jennifer!'

'Some PONIES??'

'Yes! A few miles this side of Newcombe Jettage I stopped for a cup of tea at a village called Dedford Ditchbury – rather an uninteresting place, I thought. But there was a notice outside a farmhouse which said "The Dundreary Riding School".'

'Daddy!!'

'But wait, Jennifer – there is more to come. I asked the waitress whether she could tell me about the Riding School. "Miss Daisy's place?" she replied. "It's going to close down, they say. Miss Daisy is to marry young Mr Cropleigh of Bassett St Giles." '

'Oh, dear – what a pity!'

'That's just what I said, Jennifer, and I told the waitress that my little girl would have liked to ride there. She agreed with me that it was a pity. Now, just as I was finishing my tea, who should come in but a girl in jodhpurs and sweater. "That will be Daisy," I said to myself, and sure enough the waitress told me that it was.'

'Do you think the café was on the telephone?' asked Jennifer's mother, carelessly.

'I rather think it must have been. Anyway, I had a little talk with Miss Dedleigh-Sirkett – for that was Daisy's full name – and learnt that what I had heard was true. She was about to dispose of her ponies, all eight of them.'

'EIGHT, Daddy?' Jennifer gasped.

'That was the number she said. She asked particularly how old you were and I told her. Then she asked me outright whether you would be wanting a pony all to yourself.'

'Oh, Daddy!!'

'Because, she said, there was *one* pony in her stable which would be *exactly* right for a girl of your age. She would never have parted with him in the ordinary way but now the time had come and she had no alternative. . . . All that she cared for was to see that each of her ponies had a good home. So I asked whether I could see the pony she had been speaking about. She readily agreed and there he was in the paddock, a piebald called Prune. And do you know, Jennifer – I bought him there and then!'

'But, darling!' protested Jennifer's mother. 'You should at least have asked to have him on trial!'

'I dare say I should. But I was rather excited at the time, having just had my interview with Sir Tracy Evans. I knew that I would be appointed – felt quite certain about it. I also knew what it would mean to you. And then the chance was too good to miss, the pony for sale and Jennifer's birthday within a few days. There was one other thing . . . a rather silly thing, really.'

'What was that, darling?'

'Well, my father was in the R.A.F., you know, and he used to talk about a character called Pilot Officer Prune. So I couldn't resist a Piebald Pony Prune – not on that day, anyway!'

'Oh, Daddy, how WONDERFUL!'

Jennifer went to bed that night the happiest girl in London, with eight ponies on her windowsill and one *real* pony, she knew, already hers. She was going to live in Dorset and everything was just perfect. If anyone had any doubts about the future it was Jennifer's mother. She remembered, as she went to sleep, that she too had heard of Pilot Officer Prune. But had he been a very *good* pilot? Or had he been, as she suspected, a very poor pilot indeed? And if that were so, would anyone have called the perfect pony, PRUNE?

# 3

# DISMOUNTED RALLY

THE Pony Club of the Port Bygone Hunt in South Dorset was run at this time by Miss Helena Nutshell and Major Bastable – who had fought (it was said) at Balaclava. The District Commissioner was the Hon. Mrs Harriet Hark-Forrard of Canterley Court, but she was seen only occasionally. It was Miss Nutshell who did most of the work, aided by Daisy, whose pupils were all members of the Club. In April that year – the year when Daisy's engagement was announced – there was to be a Dismounted Rally. There was the usual muddle about date, time and place, but the children were finally assembled in the Parish Hall at Snaffleford. There were diagrams and a blackboard, and Daisy was there to operate the film projector; for the lecture was to be followed by a movie about the Badminton Horse Trials.

'I shall begin,' said Miss Nutshell, 'with a few words for the beginners. The advice I always give them is this: don't be afraid of your pony! If you are a little nervous to begin with, it is perfectly natural and nothing to be ashamed of. You will soon get over it and gain confidence. In the meanwhile, it is important to seem more confident, perhaps, than you are. Give the impression that you have trained a dozen ponies already. Be friendly but firm, establishing the right relationship from the outset. In nearly every case you will find that the pony will do as you want. It sometimes happens, of course, that a pony has been hopelessly mishandled by a previous owner, and that may mean trouble – both for you and for the pony. Ordinarily, however, it should be enough to observe two basic rules. First, you must make it clear from the start that *you* are in charge. Second, your firmness must never be brutal. Be patient, keep to a regular routine and don't be discouraged by a few failures. Some early mishaps are to be expected, but don't brood on them or decide, in a fit of temper, to give up riding altogether.

'I wonder now whether anyone present can tell us what the Aids are? To begin with, how many are there? Susan? Deirdre? Clare? . . .'

While all the Pony Club children were attending this lecture at the Parish Hall, Daisy's ponies were left to their own devices. What did they decide to do? They held a Rally of their own, with Old Smokey as the lecturer. It so happened, moreover, that he chose much the same subject as Miss Nutshell – the same subject but looked at from a different point of view. When the other ponies were all gathered together in the corner of the paddock, Smokey told them that his lecture would be on Child Management for Beginners.

'I shall assume,' said Smokey, 'that you have a child of your own, and that she is your first. Some of you, I know, have had a child before. For them this talk will be a Revision of what they ought to know. Others will be going to their first home – and I hope indeed that it will turn out to be a good start to a successful career.'

'Mine is all arranged!' interrupted the intolerable

Prune. 'I am to go next month to a country residence called Windfall Orchard. The child is called Jennifer and I shall be her first. . . .'

'How funny!' exclaimed Unbeatable. 'Do you think you will be there for more than a week?'

'Look here, I'd have you know that – '

'QUIET,' roared Smokey. 'Silence! No more interruptions, please. And keep your questions until I have finished. Is that understood? Right, then. Now pay attention and don't fidget.'

'HUSH!' said Prune, looking at Unbeatable.

'I'll assume,' said Smokey, repeating himself, 'that you have a child of your own and that she is your first. (When interrupted I always go right back to the beginning and start afresh.) You may be a little nervous at first, but that is perfectly natural, nothing to be ashamed of. You will soon get over it and gain confidence. In the meanwhile it is a good plan to seem more confident than you are. Allow it to be thought that you must have trained a dozen girls already. Be firm but friendly, establishing the right sort of relationship from the outset. In almost every instance you will find that the child will do as you want, being only too anxious to keep you in a good mood. There are children, however, who are stubborn or lazy; often the fault of some previous pony. Should you come to see that your little girl has been hopelessly mishandled and is liable to neglect her chief duty (which is, of course, to look after you), there is only one thing to do. What is it, somebody?'

'You could kick in the stable door,' suggested Mischief helpfully.

'Quite wrong,' replied Smokey. 'The right answer, now, Unbeatable?'

'You should write at once to the British Horse Society.'

'Correct, and this is something you all need to know. In years gone by, before the Society was formed, horses and ponies had to endure all sorts of discomforts. But a group of far-sighted horses came together with the object of preventing future neglect. With a Derby Winner in the chair and several well-known thoroughbreds on the platform, it was agreed unanimously to form a Society for the protection of equine interest. This was done, the first meeting was held in the Albert Hall, and the Society is now firmly established, with branches in every county. See that your subscription is paid and see that you know the address of your branch secretary.' Smokey paused while the ponies nodded to each other, evidently intending to insist on their rights.

'I'll suppose now that you have comfortable quarters, regular and varied meals, clean water and plenty of extras. You have made it clear that you expect the highest standards and that nothing less will do. There remains the question of exercise. You will usually find it convenient to take this daily in the company of the little girl you have engaged to look after you. Exercise can be interesting and pleasant provided you make it clear that *you* are in charge and that all major decisions must be left to you. Be firm, be patient, and don't be discouraged by a few failures. Some early mishaps are to be expected and you should not brood on them or decide, in a fit of temper, not to be ridden at all. Before taking exercise for the first time you should make friends with the child, nuzzle up to her and nibble the lapel of her jacket. Give the child confidence, remembering that a nervous child can be a nuisance, tugging at the reins and squealing. But the friendly relationship need not prevent you instilling, as you must do, the habit of obedience. Now, to obtain obedience, we have the four AIDS. Can any pony tell me what they are?'

'The Head,' said Dunblane.

'The Teeth,' said Mischief.

'The Hooves,' said Prune.

'The Whinny,' said Spice.

'And what use do we make of the head?'

'It is used,' said Dunblane, 'to steer in the chosen direction.'

'Quite right,' said Smokey approvingly. 'The head is used to steer in the direction you choose. You may want to go where the grass is sweet and juicy. You might want to have a few words with another pony. You may well have tired of the exercise, deciding that the moment has come to return to the stable. Whatever your decision, you should turn your head in the appropriate direction and move, without needless haste, towards the destination which happens to meet your mood of the moment. You will presently feel a violent tugging on the reins, suggesting that your little girl has some other idea in mind. Fond as you may be of the child, attentive as she may be at feeding time, you will realize that to humour her would be fatal. So you ignore the reins and move quietly and firmly as planned. Should there be further tugging, accompanied perhaps by kicks and cries of rage, it is usually sufficient to shake your head. When you feel a nervous clutch at your mane, you will know that the hint has been taken and that your "No!" is regarded as final. Suppose now that you have reached the corner of the field in which you have decided to graze, you reach down and take the first mouthful of grass, thus catching the child by surprise. She is pulled forward by the reins and may, at this stage, begin to kick and scream afresh. To this the correct answer is to bring your head up again sharply, hitting her in the nose. There is no need to be bad-tempered or brutal. Use just enough force to indicate that your decision has been taken and that grazing, not trotting, is to be the agreed policy. Don't show any sign of weakness at this point. Any wavering will be sensed by the child who may try to re-open an argument which has in fact been settled. Be firm and remember the maxim: USE YOUR HEAD.

'In nine cases out of ten, use of the first Aid will be sufficient. But ill-trained children can be obstinate. With these, and on rare occasions even with well-mannered children, you may have to resort to the second Aid; the Hooves. You have decided, let me suppose, that the time has come to part; not permanently, of course, but for the time being. A temporary separation can be brought about in several ways, the simplest being the swerve. Whether at the little girl's suggestion, or according to your own whim, you are galloping (let us say) North. At the chosen moment you abruptly alter course, proceeding either East or West. The child you are training will continue in the original course, approximately, and sail over your withers. Moving about N.E.

or N.W. she will land in the grass or mud. Some ponies scamper away after this showdown, knowing that any little girl should enjoy a game of hide-and-seek. Others graze quietly in a corner of the field, preferring that the incident should be regarded as closed. On the whole, the second plan is to be preferred. Your point made, you can let bygones be bygones. The hooves can also be used in other ways. With exceptionally ill-mannered children, whose whole attitude is selfish and wilful, you may have to rear and buck or even resort to an alternation of both. To rear you bring the forefeet off the ground and balance gracefully on the hindlegs, allowing the child to slide off backwards. To buck you can raise the *hindlegs* off the ground, encouraging the child to proceed over your head. Or else you can bound gaily upwards on *all four* legs, sending the child heavenward. The drawback, in theory, to this last method is that the child might descend (eventually) into the saddle. In practice, however, this rarely happens. To move on for a few paces would seem a reasonable precaution, but it seldom proves necessary.

'On the subject of bucking, rearing and swerving, you must realize that these antics are used only in the last resort and only, of course, in the open field. In the stable yard or loosebox you should follow a more dignified policy, remembering that you can hurt yourself in kicking brickwork or timber. Even in the yard, however, you may need to show who is master. This is best done with the teeth, an occasional nip being quite enough as a reminder. It is in the stable again that you will use the fourth aid; the whinny. By this you call the child's attention to some instance of neglect. She has been slow, perhaps, in fetching your bran, the hay-net is half empty or you have accidentally overturned the water bucket. It may be, perhaps, that you miss the pony who usually occupies the loosebox next to yours. Whatever the grievance, make her realize at once that her fault has been observed and that you will tolerate no further slackness. Once she is allowed to get away with slipshod work, there is no knowing where it will all end. Make it clear from the outset that only the best will do.

'Once the proper relationship has been established, you should behave, in general, with consideration and kindness. Plan each ride so as not to bore the little girl, choosing varied paths and returning, where possible, by a different way. She should enjoy the walk as much (or *almost* as much) as you do. So choose different places for grazing and different ponies to visit. You may think that you are doing her a kindness in taking her with you, but remember how useful she can be in opening the gates. And now, a word of warning about traffic. All roads of above the smallest width are liable to carry traffic; lorries, cars and motor-cycles. If you have grown up near the highway you are probably well accustomed to the noise and smell. Cars rush by and you know that they won't harm you. Motor-cycles make that roaring sound and you are simply not interested. You could easily gain a reputation for being quiet in traffic. But that is not the reputation you should want to have. Saddle yourself with that story and you will have to hack for miles on slippery roads. Every Pony Club Rally will be held eight miles away and Bridget (or whatever her name is) will be told to ride there. Why? Because you are said to be good in traffic. So make it clear from the start that a single car will make you leap into the air, that a slow-moving truck is enough to give you hysterics and that a noisy motor-cycle could leave you dead of heart failure. What is the point, you ask? Why, to ensure that you should travel to the Rally in a borrowed trailer hitched to Farmer Hall's Land-Rover. Why hack when you can travel in comfort?

'Having arrived at the Rally or Hunter Trials in your trailer, you will be expected, on occasion, to compete with other ponies in jumping. It would be easy, of course, to avoid this altogether. You could say, in effect: "Trotting – yes; Cantering – sometimes; Galloping – very occasionally; Jumping – NO!!" With legs thrust outward and ears back, you could make your position clear. Would that, however, be wise? You do not wish, remember, to part with a girl you have trained to look after you. You may not find another as suitable and, even if you do, she too must be trained for her humble role. And yet the pony who fails to jump may well have to resign his stable to a pony who jumps at the drop of a horse shoe. Is the alternative, then, to become a known show jumper whose clear rounds become monotonous? No, that is to lead a far more energetic life than is likely to suit your taste. Here, in short, is the opportunity for compromise. Gain the reputation of a pony who can jump when he feels like it. This will keep your child in a state of suspense and hope, doing all she can to prevent you feeling sulky on the day of the competition. Make it clear to her that you can be coaxed into an average performance but that any opposition to your wishes will bring on a maddening exhibition of Equine Perversity. After demonstrating briefly that you *can* jump, you will then swerve past one obstacle, knock down the second and refuse the third. ('What is Equine Perversity?' asked Prune in a whisper. '*You* should know!' muttered Brighty, and added 'Hush!')

'I must not end this lecture,' said Smokey, 'without some advice concerning these strenuous meetings which last all day, or which (in extreme cases) can last two days or even three. They begin with miles across country, climax with simply hours of senseless games like musical gates, and end with a long trudge home in the gathering darkness. You will have decided, at an early hour, that this sort of thing is not up your paddock. More is being asked of you than is reasonable, nor is this the sort of effort for which you had bargained in the first place. For the one day you must carry it off as well as you can but you have decided, let us agree, that it must *never* happen again. How are you to make this clear? It is really quite simple. End the return journey at a very slow walk and lead the way into your stable. After unsaddling, your little girl will bring you your supper. Take no notice of either food or drink, standing motionless and exhausted, your head drooping and your tail tucked in. Your child will be seriously alarmed. Hurrying into the house she will sprint back with rugs and hot-water bottles. She will make a bran mash, adding a bottle of "Pony" ale. She will coax you with carrots and apples. It will gladden your heart to realize how fond of you she has become. But you must firmly refuse

everything, assuming the martyr's crown and clinging to it. Show no sign whatever of recovery until she talks of telephoning the veterinary surgeon. Then, and not until then, you can relax to the point of eating half a carrot, listlessly dropping the other half. She will redouble her efforts and offer you some sugar. Take a little and then hang your head afresh. When she talks of the telephone again, take a mouthful of hay and allow her to think that you have an even chance of survival. Keep her flapping round the stable for three or four hours in all, with her anxiety at fever pitch. Revive a little, finally, and allow her to get some sleep.

'Is all this too difficult? It is certainly not easy. For some hours you will have to refuse everything you like just at a time when you need it most. For the same period you must witness your little girl's anxiety, your inclination being to end the scene with some sign of reassurance. But the play-acting will be worthwhile. You will overhear her explaining that you did your level best to compete but that the whole effort was really beyond your strength. No pony can do *more* than his best and your final exhaustion was all too obvious. Reluctantly, sadly, she will have crossed all future engagements of this type out of her engagement book. She will have concluded that you are too young (or possibly too old) for such strenuous events. Having done it once, you will never be called upon to do it again. You can reasonably hope, after this, to live happily ever after.'

That was the end of the lecture and all the other ponies applauded loudly. They had been careful not to interrupt, knowing that Smokey would begin all over again, and they told each other afterwards that Smokey's ideas were quite brilliant. 'That scheme now of pretending to fall ill – a wonderful plan, don't you think?'

But that was the part that others felt doubtful about. 'But could one actually *refuse* sugar?' asked Dunblane. 'I mean, if it was actually *there* under your nose?' Spice looked dubious and Mischief said flatly that he couldn't. They all agreed, however, that the idea was, in theory, among the best they had ever heard.

Meanwhile, over in the Parish Hall at Snaffleford, Miss Nutshell was ending her lecture at about the same time.

'Just before this meeting I was asked a question which I just have time to answer. What do you do if your pony is just lazy, trying to shirk at every jump and pretending to be worn out before the Rally is half finished? I am very glad that someone – it was Susan, wasn't it? – asked that question because the problem crops up every year. And the answer is simple, although a bit unkind. As the pony begins to give trouble or refuse you get someone to come up behind him with a broomstick. It just needs the one good whack, most probably, and he will decide to behave. Never forget that it is you, not he, that is in charge.'

# 4

# THE PONY CLUB CAMP

By the time of the Melbury Horticultural Show, which happens in May, several of the ponies had gone to a new home. Unbeatable went, inevitably, to Clare Rounding. Prune we already know about; he found a fine new stable at Windfall Orchard. For young Jennifer any pony was better than none; or so she thought for the first few weeks. Brighty was to go to Sally Bopwith, who wanted a second pony (spoilt child that she was). Dunblane, the last pony any sane person could want, was in fact one of the earlier ones to go, being acquired as a birthday present for Diana Dashwood. How Diana's aunt, Mrs Bifocal, could ever have thought Dunblane a suitable mount for Diana must remain a mystery. That is nevertheless what happened and it would be hard to say which was the more embarrassed, the girl or the pony. The aunt was alone in believing that her choice represented an astute stroke of business. Diana, for her part, thought that the old lady must be completely dotty; which, as a matter of fact, she is. Diana rechristened Dunblane 'The Dismal Dumpling' and that was soon the name by which he was known. But of all the ponies at the Dundreary School, the most unlucky was poor Mischief. And here again we are faced by an apparently hopeless problem. Why, in heaven's name, should Mrs Overwaite have chosen Mischief as the right pony for Deirdre? To this question I have no answer. All we know is that the arrangement was made and marked the beginning of a most unpromising partnership.

It was at the Melbury Show that the ponies still with Daisy met those who had already found another stable. All the Pony Club was there and it was a great opportunity for gossip. Each wanted to know how the others had fared. There was also talk about the Pony Club Camp, which always happened in August. And, more immediately, there were the actual events to discuss; which pony had done well or badly, and what the chances were of Unbeatable winning the highest number of points. So far as that went, Unbeatable had at least nothing to fear from Mischief. By the last day of the Show that pony's heart was ready to break.

'Hard luck, Mischief! You were a good fourth, mind you, and there *might* have been a rosette going. I had a yellow rosette once when *I* was fourth – "Reserve", you know. Well, we can't win every time, can we?'

Dunblane, the pony now known as the Dismal Dumpling, was, as usual, making matters worse. Mischief had just come back to the collecting ring after the Junior Jumping event, won (of course) by Unbeatable, with Clare Rounding.

'I didn't think Deirdre was being particularly helpful. But for her, old horse, you might have been third. That's what *I* thought, anyway, and several of the other ponies said the same. Did I ever tell you about the time *I* was third?'

'Yes, Dumpling, you did,' snapped Mischief. 'Often! And no one would know, from the way you tell it, that it was the Leading Rein Class, with four ponies entered and one of them scratched.'

Mischief spoke bitterly, choking back a sob. It was bad enough to come in with eight faults. But to be treated as a fellow duffer by this Dumpling creature turned gloom into agony.

'No need to be rude,' replied Dumpling. 'I was only trying to cheer you up.'

The two ponies stood hitched to the rail while their two small girls had left the ring. Mischief's handicap was that sack-like creature Deirdre Overwaite, who had gone to buy herself some candy floss. As for Dumpling's partner, Diana Dashwood, she had run off to cry behind the tent devoted to Garden Implements. For her, and for Mischief, the day had been disastrous.

'You'll do better next year,' Dumpling continued unfeelingly. 'If Paleface, say, were to go down with glanders, you might be third, with a green rosette; which I myself have had only once.'

'And if all the other ponies were to drop dead, *you* would win the sash of honour,' said Mischief. In no other circumstance, to be sure, would such a result have been likely. Dumpling was, in every way, the Pony Club Bore. But Mischief's chances, with Deirdre up, were little better. This wretched child would never give him sufficient rein; and each attempt at a fence ended with a jabbed mouth and another pole on the ground. Hopeless in the saddle and not much better in the stable, Deirdre was the subhuman equivalent of the Dismal Dumpling. So poor Mischief was literally saddled with a sausage-shaped, mouth-jabbing and selfish child, the joke of the

Pony Club. To make matters worse, she proposed to take him to the Pony Club Camp.

The camp that year was to be at Mickleby Moorside. The ponies would be in a paddock, the girls under canvas and the meals served in Farmer Woodcock's barn. The organizing committee members would be Miss Helena Nutshell, Major Bastable (who charged, you will remember, with the Light Brigade) and Mrs Kewside, who would see to the catering. They could expect a visit from the Commissioner, The Hon. Mrs Hark-Forrard, and there was pretty certain to be that film on the Ponies of Paraguay. For a lively pony like Mischief some of the games would have been rather fun; nor would he have minded the all-day Trek or the Visitors' Day. But what could he do in partnership with Dreary Deirdre? She would oversleep and they would be late for inspection. She would fail to slacken the guy ropes and the tentpole would fall on her. She would have forgotten her raincoat and might catch cold when it drizzled. There would be a line of smashed fences, with Major Bastable muttering that there had been less damage at the storming of the Malakoff. There would be Miss Nutshell screaming, '*Will* you *make* your pony canter?' while Deirdre tugged at the reins. Finally there would be the return to the Pony Lines with Dumpling saying, 'Hard luck, old horse! A bit off colour today? I have the same trouble sometimes. Did I ever tell you about the time when . . .?'

The camp was very much what Mischief thought it would be, but Mrs Harriet Hark-Forrard, who appeared on the second day, shook up the morning session by calling, 'Change ponies!' She did not say who should change with what, but Diana was on Mischief before most people had so much as looked around. There was a scampering and a squealing and a lengthening and shortening of stirrup leathers, in the midst of which Deirdre, wandering aimlessly around, found a riderless pony. It was Dumpling and she managed, at the third attempt, to place herself in the saddle. A minute later the ride moved off, circled left, circled right, quitted stirrups and were told to trot. There was a mutual sympathy between Deirdre and Dumpling. Here, the girl felt, was a pony which would never do the unexpected – would never, for preference, do anything at all. She felt, for the first time, confident and safe. Dumpling, for his part, felt relieved to be rid of Diana, a girl who was always urging him to jump ditches and fences, scramble up banks and wade through streams. Deirdre, now, was less demanding. She expected him to trot when the others did and even canter when the time for cantering had apparently come. But that was all she expected and more than she got. For Deirdre the pony Dumpling began to show a tolerance bordering on affection.

Between Mischief and Diana there was, by contrast, a real romance. It would seem that they had been friends from the beginning of time. Each knew what the other was thinking and anticipated what the others would do. It was not a question of riding or being ridden; they floated together in a golden haze, danced to the music of the trumpets which no one had actually blown.

'What do you think you are doing?' asked Miss Nutshell sarcastically.

'Really, child!' protested Major Bastable.

But Diana did not even hear them, and Mischief's hooves were not touching the ground. Each had lived for this moment of discovery, the finding of the perfect partner. Each knew that separation might follow, that they might never come together again, that the minutes they had must be lived as if they were the last. Sharing their brief heaven, they behaved very badly indeed. 'Get that pony under control!' shouted the Crimean Major. 'You are upsetting the whole ride!' wailed Mrs Hark-Forrard. 'Stop that circus act, Diana!' screamed Miss Helena Nutshell. So annoyed was the Major with Mischief's prancing about that he did something he should not have done. He tried to bring Mischief back to earth with his whip, used quite smartly on the pony's rump. Unfortunately, his wrath was more impressive than his eyesight. His whip fell on the wrong pony – on the wretched Dumpling, who happened to be standing where Mischief had been a few seconds before. The crack of the whip was enough to bring Mischief under control. It was from the back of a perfectly behaved pony that Diana made her apologies. 'I'm so sorry, Mrs Hark-Forrard. This pony is a little fresh.' But the committee members were not listening. They were gazing in blank surprise at a moving object in the distance; a dwindling speck which was passing from the middle distance into the background, out of the background towards the horizon, over the horizon and out of the picture. It was Dumpling and Deirdre, moving as neither had ever moved before.

Reading the last two sentences I feel that I may have

misled the reader, giving Dumpling a turn of speed he could not possibly have had. In point of fact, his gallop was nothing remarkable. It came as a surprise, nevertheless, to those who knew him best; which is why they stared after him at a moment when they could perhaps have tried to head him off. It also came as a surprise to Deirdre, who clung to his mane, staying somehow in the saddle until such time as he should choose to halt. It was a good twenty-five minutes before that idea occurred to him, and they had by that time covered some four or five miles. Miss Nutshell finally came up with them near Bingley Common, where Deirdre was in the pond and Dumpling grazing calmly on the bank. By the time they were all back in camp, Deirdre had the symptoms of a nasty cold. She was put to bed in the farmhouse with a hot drink and a hot-water bottle.

Back in the pony lines, Dumpling made the most of his adventure. 'Actually,' he explained to the other ponies, 'I am not at all keen on this Riding School routine. I do better, really, in a Point-to-Point. Take this morning's run, for example. I dare say one or two others here could have equalled my time over the given distance – some could, others couldn't – but would any other pony (I ask myself) be as fresh as I am at the end of the day? Stamina, that is what so many ponies lack! Good to look at, some of them, keen to jump, but show them the open country, the far horizons – and where *are* they?' At that moment, before he could answer his own question, poor Dumpling collapsed in a heap and lay there until morning. Completely exhausted, he stayed in the pony

lines for the next three days, having his breakfast in bed and telling all visitors, in a feeble voice, that his life was drawing peacefully to its close.

With Deirdre and Dumpling on the sick list, it was inevitable that Diana should ride Mischief. She was still riding him when Visitors' Day came, with a display for parents and friends. On the previous evening Diana had a talk with Deirdre, who was recovering but not expected to compete. Diana came straight to the point by proposing that they should swap ponies.

'I get on well with Mischief,' she said, 'and you are far happier on Dunblane.' (She was careful to use the pony's real name.)

'All very fine,' Deirdre replied, 'but Mischief is a far better pony.'

'Mischief is more promising *as a show jumper*,' Diana admitted. 'But aren't you forgetting your own cross-country performance on Dunblane? Do you know what I thought at the time?'

'No, Diana, do tell me,' pleaded Deirdre.

'I thought that you would do well in a Three Day Event!'

'No – *really*?'

'You were splendid. I'll never forget how you kept in the saddle. Hill and dale, hedges and ditches – you took 'em all in your stride.'

'Well, I did come off in the end. . . .'

'Ah,' said Diana, 'but that was miles away, after you had been galloping for hours.'

'I didn't know,' admitted Deirdre, 'that old Dumpling had it in him.'

'Nor did I!' said Diana eagerly. 'The fact is, I have not got the best out of that pony. It needed a better rider to show what he is really capable of.'

'Oh, no!' protested Deirdre. 'You are far better than I am!'

'Well, I'll admit I thought I was. But I realize now that Dunblane has great possibilities – with you! *I* could never do much with him, but *you* understand his character.'

'Nice of you to say so. . . . All right, Diana, let's swap! Your parents and mine will be here tomorrow. It can all be fixed then, before the Display!'

The exchange was agreed without much argument and the Display was a great success. Mischief was an easy winner in musical gates and pushed Firefly (ridden by Rachel Rossetti) to third place in the obstacle race. Then came the Jumping event, which had always meant an easy victory for Unbeatable (and Clare Rounding). But Mischief sailed effortlessly over every jump and there was a final jump-off between the two. Twice the jumps were raised and then – to everyone's surprise – Unbeatable refused at the brick wall. Three minutes later Mischief did a last clear round and received the red rosette. The happiest girl that day was Diana and the happiest pony was Mischief. Deirdre had been terribly useful giving out the programmes and Dumpling had been ridden in turn by the younger brothers and sisters. That evening, back in the pony lines, he told the other ponies about it. Not every pony, he pointed out, has the patience for this sort of work.

'It's a sort of knack,' he admitted, 'which a few ponies have. The tricky part is when you have walked across the paddock and have to go back again. To circle round smoothly, so that the child doesn't fall off, is something of an art. There's more in it than you might think. Even *before* that, there can be a crisis – we had one this afternoon. There is a point, halfway (or *nearly* halfway) across the paddock, when the child realizes that it's mother has been left behind at the starting line. This is called, technically, the point of no return. Well, that was where the trouble began. I had sensed it coming, mind you. One develops a sort of instinct as the result of experience. But for that, things might have been serious. It occurred to me at the time that a rosette for saving life would have been a nice gesture. Did I ever tell you, Mischief, about the time I was third . . .?'

But Mischief wasn't listening. Diana was patting his neck and stroking his mane and saying, 'You are the most wonderful pony in the whole world!'

Overhearing this, Dumpling muttered, 'There's no accounting for tastes!'

## 5

## SPICE GOES HUNTING

SPICE was still with Daisy when the autumn came and then the winter. The smallest of the ponies, he was not up to the weight of the older girls, nor was he quiet enough for some of the younger ones. He was a good pony, nevertheless, and Daisy was asked one day whether he could go out hunting with Susan Harker, whose own pony had gone lame. This was agreed and Spice was very excited about it. Knowing nothing of the hunting field, he asked Smokey to tell him the 'Do's and Don'ts'.

'Well, young Spice,' said the old pony. 'Be up early on the day of the Hunt, which you'll find easier if you remember to have a good rest the day before. The next thing is to ensure that your child is properly groomed and smartly turned out. See that her hat is brushed, her tie on straight, her collar clean and her shoes polished. Some child owners put a bandage on the girl's pony-tail the evening before, damping the hair beforehand. If you do this – and in your place I shouldn't bother – don't tie the bandage too tight; otherwise she may be sore in the morning. If she has forgotten anything in the excitement of the moment, remind her with a nip and send her back for it. After all, you want the child to be a credit to you. So keep her up to the mark.'

'Of course, Smokey. How right you are!' said Spice.

'One other thing: hack slowly to the Meet, even if your child should want to hurry. Once there, you will probably want to have a word with the other ponies, especially your old friends. Perhaps the little girl – Susan, did you say? – may have other ideas. If she has, remind her sharply that she is neglecting your welfare. "You haven't tightened my girth, you nit!" is a good beginning, although it's not easy to put it across. If she is still excited, walk her in a circle until the Hunt moves off. When this happens, keep in rear, out of harm's way. And, last of all, whatever you do, never get in front of the hounds!'

Spice had forgotten half the good advice by the day of the Hunt. He and Susan were there, nevertheless, when the Hunt began; and Susan luckily knew more about hunting than he did. It was, after all, her third time out. She and Spice kept back at first, very much as Smokey advised, and they presently joined a group of horses at the covert side. They saw nothing for what seemed a long time and heard nothing except the noise of hounds crashing about in the undergrowth. Then, very faintly, came the View-Holloa, followed by the horn sounding, 'Gone away.' The sound came from the *far* side of the wood and all the horses near Spice set off at a canter, going back the way they had come. They circled round to the point at which the fox broke cover. By the time Susan and Spice had arrived there, the hounds had disappeared from the scene, followed by most of the field. Susan could recognize some movement about three fields away. There was a riderless horse pausing for lunch in the next field but one, and a farm terrier was having hysterics in the foreground. At Susan's suggestion, Spice set off at a canter in what appeared to be the right direction.

Coming to the first gate which stood open, Susan noticed for the first time that there was no other rider behind her. She realized with a sinking heart that it was her duty to close all gates after the Hunt had passed. She remembered that from a Pony Club lecture, and remembered too that there is a drill for gate-shutting, one which depends upon the rider having a whip and the pony some considerable practice in reining back. Susan had lost her whip ten days before, so Spice halted after passing each gate, leaving her to dismount and close the thing. 'Good practice for her!' Spice said to himself. 'Might help her some day to win the run-and-mount competition!' By the time Susan had closed eight or nine gates she had learnt that every other gate has to be lifted bodily and that every fourth gate lacks hinges altogether. For half an hour she rode on, cheered occasionally by the distant glimpse of a horse, and convinced, from a study of the hoof-marks and manure, that a number of horses must recently have passed that way. Presently she noticed that all was silent except for the distant barking of sheep dogs. There was nobody about and even the hoof-marks seemed, surely, fewer. What there were led rather to the left and into the fields. When the path forked, therefore, Susan branched left and followed it at the trot. But now she found that there were no hoof-marks at all! Pressing on desperately, she found that she was approaching a wood. A pale November sun lit up the empty landscape and even the sheep dogs had forgotten at last what it was they were barking about. Susan realized that she was utterly and completely lost.

But just at the moment that Susan was beginning to

whimper, she suddenly realized that she was *not* lost; nor, for that matter, was she out of the Hunt. Far from that, the sounds of the Hunt were to be heard again and were getting nearer. She guessed that the Huntsman had cast back and that the hounds were coming straight towards her. The horn sounded now from the far side of the wood. Stopping just short of where the undergrowth began, Susan and Spice waited to see what would happen next. A scarlet coat appeared at the far corner of the wood to the right, some black coats somewhere to the left. The hounds were working through the wood, coming in Susan's direction, and one of them gave tongue. It was on the scent, and then the others joined in. Susan was fairly trembling with excitement and so was Spice. Then she saw something move in the bracken. What was it? Could it be ... ? And it *was*! There appeared a magnificent dog fox, tired by the look of it and just about to break cover. Out he came, bounding into the open, and the scarlet coated gentleman was suddenly there at the covert side.

'Holloa!' screamed Susan wildly.

'SHUT UP, YOU LITTLE FOOL!' shouted the Whip, and galloped back the way he had come. Two or three minutes later came the proper View-Holloa, and then everything happened at once. The hounds poured out of the wood in a frenzy of excitement, with the Huntsman's horn sounding above the din. The Whip collected a stray hound over to the left and drove it after the rest. Horses came thundering up on all sides, and the hunt was on!

Susan was in the first flight but kept a little to one side,

out of the way of the rest. Spice pounded along after the Field Master, showing a great turn of speed for his size. There was a bank in front but he scrambled over it in a flash. There was a fence now – he was up and over. There was a big field ahead, the hounds in full cry and the fox in view. Susan could see that the hounds were right on the fox's brush. . . . A moment later and they had done it! Fairly bowled over in the open! Susan saw that several men in scarlet had dismounted and that the hounds were gathered round one of these in a final frenzy. Susan drew rein and Spice stood there proudly, the pony that was in at the death. Susan heard her name called, and gave Spice's reins to Judith while she ran over to the Field Master. 'Well done!' he said as he blooded her. 'You should enter that pony of yours for the Grand National!' As other members of the Pony Club came up, they called out 'Well done!' in their turn. But Susan patted her pony's neck and said, 'Well done, Spice!' They had both forgotten by then how much it had been a matter of luck.

It was still early in the day and the Hunt was to draw the Priory Woods. Hounds moved off in that direction, followed by the field, and Susan, left to herself, would have hunted on until the day's end. But Spice remembered some last-minute advice he had been given by Smokey. 'Don't go on too long!' he had urged. 'By 1.30 at latest, you should assert yourself, put your hoof down.' And this was now what Spice did. Susan could squeeze and kick as much as she liked, but there was only one direction in which he was prepared to move. Homewards! After a short argument, Susan came to realize that the pony was right and that her parents, had they been present, would have said the same. So the ride home began, several of the Pony Club heading for

Dedford Ditchbury and all the children having plenty to talk about. Back in the Riding School Stable Susan rubbed her pony down, examined his hooves and removed some thorns from his legs. He was fed and watered and made comfortable for the night. Spice also had what he wanted just as much – a friend with whom to discuss the events of the day. For the evening is the time when you can have the Hunt all over again but under better conditions, with cold and fatigue a thing of the past and the story reshaping itself so as to make you (whether child or pony) the central figure in a drama of endurance and heroism. Now each can enjoy the Hunt as it should have been, with triumphs and laughter in their proper proportion, with rivals outwitted and friends admiring, with virtue rewarded and a happy ending already assured.

For young Susan the story took this form, 'I *knew* somehow, Mummy, that hounds would be drawing Hogben's Wood. So when the field was trailing over to Withenshaw and back – they found nothing *there* of course – I rode over the warren, past the woodman's cottage, and there, sure enough, the Hunt arrived. Gosh, it was exciting! I could hardly believe my luck when I saw that fox come out of the bracken. I very nearly called out! ("But I hope you didn't?" said her father.) Oh, *no*! That could have frightened him back into the covert. I waited for the Whip to come up and it was *he* who gave the View-Holloa. Then the hounds came and we all tore after them, flat out until the kill. Spice and I were right up in front, just behind Captain Hackenham-Helltoyou. The Master said I had done terribly well. I didn't see Sylvia Greenish until ten minutes later, and Judith came up later still, with Michael and Sally Bopwith right behind.'

Out in the stables, meanwhile, Spice has his own story to tell and Smokey is the first to hear it.

'I wouldn't let Susan hurry over towards Withenshaw. Indeed, I can't think what the Master was thinking of! Who ever found a fox *there*? At Barton's Orchard, maybe; at Martleshams, perhaps, but at Withenshaw – never. So I stayed around Hogben's Wood. And it was there, sure enough, that they found.'

'Quite right, old pony!' replied Smokey. 'Go easy at first. Hold back until the right moment comes!'

'What a horn-blowing there was,' the story went on. 'What a crashing and a bashing! Then, suddenly, there was the fox. . . . I was after him like a flash!'

'But you didn't get in front of the hounds, I hope?' asked Smokey anxiously.

'Well, not actually in front of them. At one point I did have to show them the way.'

'Quite so,' said Smokey. 'Our eyes are farther off the ground. We can see while a hound is merely trying to smell.'

'But don't imagine,' Spice concluded, 'that I would ever try to do the hounds' work for them. Shouldn't dream of it! If they don't mind occasionally accepting a hint, they are welcome to all the credit that may be going. Well, it's time for bed now. You know something, Smokey? I think this is the best day's hunting I ever had!'

## 6

# BRIGHTY'S CHRISTMAS

AT the time of the Pony Club Camp Brighty's future had been all agreed. He was to be Sally Bopwith's second pony, Blackie being her first – and Blackie had come near to being the junior jumping champion at the Midsummer Show. Sally's idea was to have a second pony, with a double chance of winning next time. The gradual dispersal, therefore, of the other ponies – Unbeatable, Prune, Mischief and Dunblane – had not depressed Brighty unduly. Sally, he knew, could not have him until the New Year, but after that he would be going to his new home, and one where there would be another pony to talk to. But horrid rumours began to circulate that summer, for Sally was known to be collecting pop records. The hunt at which Susan was blooded was the last, in fact, at which Sally was seen. Months before that, however, all Brighty's worst fears had been confirmed. The wretched girl had fallen a victim to something called the Twist, had become an addict and was thought incurable. Blackie eventually left her in disgust, her Pony Club membership lapsed and her stable was turned into a Rumpus Room. As a show competitor Sally was finished and so, for the moment, was Brighty. You would have supposed that a pony with his name would be full of high spirits, always whinnying some merry snatch of song. He whinnied all right, being very noisy in that way, but he did it in a listless and dejected tone. For poor Brighty there seemed to be no future at all.

Although Sally rode occasionally even in November, the idea of her having a *second* pony was abandoned as early as August. Soon afterwards, early in September, Brighty jumped the paddock rails one evening and disappeared. Daisy Dedleigh-Sirkett searched the countryside but without success. Brighty was never found, and for the good reason that he had gone to Port Bygone and found himself a job as a beach pony. It was nearly the end of the season but the weather held and the beach remained busy until the end of the month. For the first few days Brighty could forget his sorrows in the novelty of his surroundings and the noise and glitter of the sea. Do you blame Brighty for his mistake? Are you inclined to doubt whether any other pony would have been so foolish? I would ask you, nevertheless, not to judge him too harshly. His had been a terrible disappointment. He fled – scarcely knowing where he went – and ended, remember, in almost the worst situation that any pony can know. As compared with a pit pony, working underground, a beach pony does at least work in daylight. There is little else, however, to commend his way of life. Squalling infants are placed on his back, ice-cream drips into his ears, toffee melts into his mane and cameras click to record his discomfort. To the end of his appointed stretch he has to plod and so back to the starting point, back and forth until the sun sets and the lights come on along the darkening promenade. Tethered in some seaside field, more sand than grass, the pony looks

back on a day of humiliation, looks forward to a day no better than the last. Gradually, as the days shorten and the sea breezes blow cold, the children become few, the ice-cream vendor ceases to shout and there is the sound of deck-chairs being stacked under cover. The beach is deserted and the season is over.

Brighty's manager was a gloomy character called Albert, who lived over the harness room at the back of the Admiral Rodney Inn. In years gone by, Port Bygone had been a real seaport, with quaysides and warehouses, bollards and barrels. And the Admiral Rodney was the Inn to which the coaches had come and where passengers had waited ashore for a favourable wind. There might have been a hundred horses stabled there in the great days and there would be room for as many now. But the beach ponies have the place almost to themselves in winter, using the last six stables on the left, where Albert (living opposite) can keep an eye on them. Any hunters stabled there, as will happen sometimes, are usually put at the other end, near the Inn itself. Poor Brighty found himself lodged here for the winter with little hay and not so much as a smell of bran. And the other ponies were poor company, never having known any other life than the one they led. But Brighty's whinnying was too much for Albert, who liked, as he said, to have his sleep. With the Innkeeper's permission, Brighty was moved to a stable quite near to the Inn. He had it to himself at first and then, much to his surprise, a racehorse arrived to share it with him. Some days passed before the racehorse would even notice that Brighty was there, but sheer boredom brought them together in a friendship which would hardly otherwise have been possible.

Arab Prince was the racehorse's name and he treated Brighty at first with a thoroughbred's condescension. He merely hinted to begin with at his proud ancestry but

Brighty's awe-stricken way of saying, 'Really?' and 'Ooh, I *say*!' and 'Good gracious!' encouraged him to become more expansive. Any horse, he admitted, might be a descendant of Eclipse ('Of course!' murmured Brighty, who wasn't) but to be a descendant of Persimmon *and* Matchem was perhaps a little unusual, more especially in a cousin of Hyperion and Tulyar. 'But good breeding,' he sighed, 'carries with it a Heavy Responsibility!' ('Just so!' said Brighty, who could not imagine why.) 'I was to have raced at Goodwood last year and would probably have won the Chesterfield Cup, but a touch of lameness led to my name being scratched. I was all right for the St Leger, though.' 'Did you *win*?' whispered Brighty in a daze of admiration. 'Well, no,' admitted the thoroughbred, 'I didn't exactly *win* . . . although everyone agreed that I *would* have won but for my jockey holding me back. I was fourth actually.' 'Then why are you *here*?' asked Brighty, bewildered. 'I'm here in hiding,' whispered Arab Prince. 'No one must know. My owner thinks I may be doped or stolen. So please don't tell anyone who I am. Keep it under your mane!' 'Of course!' stuttered Brighty. 'I won't say a word, and good luck, old horse, at Doncaster!'

Brighty could keep a secret and did but Arab Prince was himself too talkative and too full of his own importance. The word got round and the very thing happened that Arab Prince's owner was trying to prevent. Late in December, two bad men, Steve and Mike, came to the 'Admiral Rodney' one dark night with a double horse trailer, believing that there were two racehorses there, one called Arab and the other, Prince. Discovering their mistake, they quietly led out the only racehorse they could find. But Brighty, noisy at the best of times, fairly screamed at the idea of losing his friend. He woke the Innkeeper, who stayed, however, in bed. 'Drat that pony,' he muttered. 'He'll have to go back to his old stable.' Said Steve to Mike, meanwhile, 'This pony will wake the parish. Let's knock him senseless!' But Mike said 'No – let's take him too.' That proved the better idea, for Brighty quietened down at once when he was led to the trailer. Within a few minutes the two bad men drove off into the night. They had covered two hundred miles by daylight, when they hid in a wood. 'Let's leave this pony here when we go,' argued Mike. 'The noise he makes may give us away.' 'That's right,' said Steve. 'One horse is enough to look after.' And when they drove on, towards evening, Brighty was left by himself in the wood. Snow began to fall and the pony began to shiver.

Without knowing where he was or where he wanted to go, Brighty trotted along the first path he saw. It led him out of the wood and across a stream, up a hill and along the other side, round an old windmill and into a lane. Presently he passed some cottages in the gathering darkness, their windows brightly lit. Inside them children were putting up streamers and balloons while their parents brought in holly by the armful. Brighty could hear the singing of a carol in the distance and realized at that moment that it was Christmas Eve! Looking into the windows as he passed he suddenly felt cold and lonely and miserable. How different it had all been a year ago! With Sally Bopwith – with the *old* Sally, that is –

Christmas would have included carrots and apples and lump sugar: with a Boxing Day Meet to follow, most likely. And by *this* Christmas she might have parted with Blackie. That would have given Brighty the thing he had always wanted – a little girl of his own. That was a Christmas present no one had ever given him: but there was little likelihood now of his getting *any* present, not so much as a handful of pony nuts! None of the villagers even heard him pass for the fallen snow had deadened the sound of his hooves. As he walked away into the darkness first one tear, then another rolled down his nose and fell into the roadway. If there was a sad pony in England that night, it was poor Brighty.

Passing through a dark wood and over the next hill, Brighty saw a house in the valley below him. There was something about the place he liked – the paddock, the outbuildings, the laughter and the lights. Drawn towards the old courtyard by an instinct he could not understand, he trotted soundlessly through a snow-covered meadow, passed quietly through an open gate and rounded the corner of a barn. There, in the courtyard, was a stable with the door left open! It was a cold night and Brighty did not hesitate for an instant. That stable, he decided, was his! A minute later he was inside and looking about him. He saw straight away that no other pony lived there and that none was expected. There was hay in the loft, to judge from the smell, and there, on the floor, was a bale of straw! It had actually been pulled out by the children, who had been finishing the crib at the Church, but Brighty could not know that. He merely thought it uncommonly thoughtful of somebody. 'Not everyone,' he said to himself, 'would have left the stable door open, just on the offchance that a stray pony might come along. But it was a kindly thought!' He kicked the straw around until he had made a bed for himself, and prepared to settle down for the night.

Before he lay down, however, there was a waving torch in the courtyard and a scampering of feet. Next came the sound of two children climbing a ladder, followed by their voices. They were immediately overhead, in the hay loft! 'Careful, Alison,' said a boy's voice. 'There's a place here where we used to pitch the hay down. You could fall through and brain yourself.'

'I know, Peter,' replied the girl, 'I won't go any farther. I'll hide the parcel here.'

'Good idea!' came the reply. 'You can sneak it in before breakfast.'

'Just what I mean to do,' said Alison. 'There was no sense in leaving it beside the tree tonight. A hockey stick is one of those things you *can't* disguise!'

'Colin will be thrilled!' said Peter.

'Do you really think so?'

'It's what he wants most in the world!'

'I do hope that's true,' was Alison's reply. 'Do you remember last Christmas – Aunt Sylvia's present?'

'A riding whip – just three weeks after Trooper broke his leg and had to be sent away. Wasn't it awful,' said Peter, 'I could have cried!'

'You *did* cry . . . and there's been no talk of another pony since.'

'I don't think it's been a good year for Daddy.'

'It hasn't,' Alison sighed. 'So I've kept jolly quiet about anything that would cost money.'

'Let's hope for better luck next year!' said Peter.

There was a clatter of footsteps, the bang of a door and the children had gone. Brighty lay down to think things over and woke to find it was morning with the church bells ringing. Christmas Day, and not even a carrot in his stocking! There was no sign of the children until after church but Brighty found some hay he could just reach. He was busy with this when he heard a door open and the sound of feet on the ladder. Alison was by herself this time, for Peter could be heard in the distance calling, 'Buck up, Alison – time for presents!' There was a scuffling in the hayloft and Brighty could hear the little girl saying, 'Bother!' to herself, and 'Oh, *where* did I put it?' and 'Drat!' A whole bale of hay fell right into the empty manger – plop! Then a second toppled on to the floor. And all the time Alison was saying, 'It *must* be here, somewhere!' And so it probably was, but Alison did not find it until later. What she found straight away was the hole in the floor through which the hay had fallen! There was a gasp and a wail of dismay and – plop! – a girl aged eight had fallen slap-bang into the manger. She did not hurt herself because of the hay that had fallen before, but she was breathless and shaken. With more hay tumbled over her eyes, she could not even see where she was. She felt her left leg – there it was! Her right leg was there too, and both arms as well. She was, in fact, none the worse. Sitting up, and brushing the hay aside, she found herself looking straight into a pony's eyes; a pony she had never seen before; a pony stabled where no pony had lived for over a year!

As for Brighty, he had never seen a little girl so exactly right in every way. Sally Bopwith had never been half as pretty and she would weigh now a great deal more. With Alison as partner, Brighty knew that he would be unbeatable for years to come, whether in musical gates or run-and-mount. Looking ahead, he could imagine the rosettes coming, one after another. Old Albert would never find him here – hundreds of miles from Port Bygone beach; and Alison's father would never know where he had come from. He had found, by his own cleverness, the perfect stable, the perfect family, and a whole loft full of hay. Best of all, there had dropped from the sky the very thing he had always dreamed of, the Christmas present that Santa Claus had so far forgotten to bring him; a little girl aged eight, weighing four stone six pounds and measuring about fourteen hooves. That was what he had wanted – a little girl for Christmas!

# 7
# THE PONY CLUB GYMKHANA

THE marriage of Daisy Dedleigh-Sirkett had been fixed for June. By the time of the Pony Club Gymkhana, which was in May, she had three ponies left. These were the three S's – Smokey, Skylark and Spice. Most people thought that Smokey was too old and some people thought that Spice was too small. Skylark, on the other hand, was admired by everyone, being the most handsome and intelligent pony of them all; and that is why Daisy could not bear to part with him. So these last three came to the Gymkhana to be ridden by the last of Daisy's pupils. And there they met with some old friends, Unbeatable and Mischief still in hot competition as show jumpers, Dunblane still giving rides to the younger children and Prune, now ridden by Jennifer, being just as idiotic as he had ever been. Because of the importance to the neighbourhood of the new Rocket Establishment at Newcombe Jettage, the Organizing Committee had asked Sir Tracy Evans to give away the prizes. This he had agreed to do, and the famous scientist was actually present from the beginning and showed a keen interest – a surprisingly keen interest – in the ponies that were competing. He soon knew them all, at least by name.

On the way over to Melbury, where the Gymkhana was held, Skylark cast a shoe. There is no blacksmith, unfortunately, at Melbury, nor indeed for miles around.

There is Mr Anvil of Port Bygone but he can never be persuaded to do any work on a Saturday afternoon – not, at least, when there is any cricket to watch. So poor Skylark's name was scratched from all events. He was left to graze quietly in a corner of the collecting ring, which allowed him to chat with his friends as they came and went. In another corner of the ring Jennifer was talking with her father.

'It's wonderful,' she said, 'to have a pony at all. I do realize how lucky I am. But Prune is certainly not going to win any prizes. I don't think he is exactly stupid, but he is either wildly excited about something he wants to do or mulishly obstinate when he ought to be doing what I want. He's a hare-brained creature, always sulking when not being completely idiotic. I can't make him jump and he'll be useless in any game like musical gates. Couldn't we get rid of him and find a better pony? I saw one just now – where was he? – the most beautiful pony I ever saw, but not competing in anything. Oh, there he is!' She pointed to Skylark. 'With a pony like that I should bring back some rosettes for the harness room! Isn't he *lovely*?'

Jennifer led the way over to the corner where Skylark was grazing. 'I see what you mean,' said her father, 'but we don't know that this one is for sale. I'll make a few inquiries if you like. In the meanwhile you are entered for Event 4, Musical Gates, and it should begin in ten minutes time. You take Prune out and show us what you can do with the pony you've got.' This conversation was overheard by Prune, who was not quite the fool he was thought to be. Useless as he was in the ordinary way, he had a streak of low cunning where his own comfort was involved. He was well treated at Windfall Orchard and did not want to give up his stable, neither to Skylark nor to any other pony. He would have been glad to have a stable companion but that, he knew, was not what Jennifer had in mind. He decided, there and then, that he must behave perfectly for once. Musical Gates would be largely a matter of luck but must also give an opportunity for quick decision, control, and speed. He would show the other ponies what he could do when he felt like it! As for Jennifer, her plea for another pony would come to nothing once she had a rosette for the one she was riding. Prune knew, of course, that Skylark was in the market and must find a home almost at once. So the situation was at once Serious and Critical. For Prune it was a case of Now or Never.

Jennifer, a fairly recent arrival in the neighbourhood, had few friends as yet in the Pony Club. Prune, by contrast, was pretty notorious. So the other children looked at Jennifer rather pityingly and several wished her luck with a snigger. 'What will Prune do *this* time?' they muttered to each other. Would he bolt back into the collecting ring or lie down in the middle of the field? Would he do a Rodeo Act or would he bite one of the judges? Life with Prune had always been a series of sad surprises but with few instances of the same disaster being exactly repeated. Uniformly absurd as he had always been, he could usually produce some Variations on the Theme. There were six gates in all, to begin with, and the competitors numbered forty-three. As soon as they were spaced round the field the music began and all the ponies began their circuit at the canter – the trot being forbidden by the rules. Only six were allowed through any gate, so there were seven competitors eliminated on the first occasion the music stopped. Poor Smokey was one of them, but Prune was not. One gate was closed after that and the next crisis removed another six. Jennifer found, to her surprise, that Prune was behaving like an angel – like an angel, moreover, who knew the rules of the game. When the gates had been reduced to four and the competitors to a dozen, Jennifer was still in the running.

It was now that Prune began to reveal a quite extraordinary talent for the game. The basic object is to be approaching a gate when the music stops. So the experienced competitors slow down when short of the gate and gallop on after passing it, so as to approach the next; once more, however, in deliberate fashion. You can't turn back, remember, and you can't do less than canter. So the advantage lies with the pony that can canter more slowly than the rest. Perhaps Prune had once practised this as a means of annoying the other ponies in the riding class. His performance, anyway, was superb. He went through the motions of cantering while barely covering the ground. It was difficult for the other children to believe that he was not actually going backwards. When there were eight riders and three gates, each admitting only two, Jennifer was again successful. So was Spice, whose small size was evidently an advantage and whose rider – a small boy who was at Melbury on a visit from another county – was evidently an old hand at the game. One gate was now closed, the last two to admit one each.

The six competitors still in the field were all pretty skilled, loitering down the long sides of the field (where the gates were) and tearing round the ends as soon as a gate was passed. Prune had developed a surprising turn of speed and was well placed when the music stopped again. With only two ponies left, there was only a single gate and that in the middle to be entered from either direction. Jennifer and Prune cantered round in the one direction, young Michael on Spice went round the other way. For the last time the music stopped. There was a wild scamper and the event was over with Jennifer the winner! She galloped back to the collecting ring with the red rosette in her mouth.

'Well!' said her father. 'I don't see what you have to complain about! Prune couldn't have done much better!'

'I know, Daddy! He was terrific! He is so stupid in the ordinary way that I couldn't believe it was the same pony. Perhaps he's a reformed character – I do hope so.'

The other girls all collected round, saying, 'Well done, Jennifer!' and 'Who would have believed it?' Many of the younger children were patting Spice, meanwhile, and saying, 'Isn't he quite adorable – with his blue rosette and all!' Spice always had his admirers; it was only their parents who were apt to say, 'But Joan will be too big for that pony by the season after next.' Among Spice's followers on this occasion was a six-year-old called Pat, there on a visit from her home in Guernsey. Her mother liked Spice almost as much as she did but made the usual comment, 'You'd outgrow him, darling, in three years at the outside.' But Pat had foreseen this objection. 'Yes, and then I'll let Neville ride him!' Neville was her younger brother, aged four, who joined in the discussion by saying, 'I want him *now*!' Pat's mother had been actually looking for a pony and she saw that Spice was very much what the family needed. 'We don't know,' she said, 'that his present owner wants to part with him.' She went off to inquire, nevertheless, and was presently seen talking to Daisy near the Refreshment Tent. 'Isn't he sweet?' asked Pat meanwhile, but there was no reply. Young Neville had found a see-saw and was being helped on to it by somebody's Nannie, whose own child was on the other end. Pat never found it easy to make Neville concentrate on the things she regarded as important.

When the last event was over Sir Tracy Evans presented the prizes. Everyone crowded round the Judges' Tent and Sir Tracy made a speech, congratulating the Committee, the Judges, the Stewards, the Competitors (both Winners and Losers), the Borough Council and the Boys' Brigade Band.

'Before I actually distribute the prizes,' he said, 'I want to tell you something of the work we are doing at Newcombe Jettage. As you all probably know, the scientists of the United States and Russia are planning a manned rocket flight to the Moon. But we here in Britain decided some years ago that the Moon is hardly worth the effort. No one can live there and it can offer us nothing, we suppose, of value. We believe, on the other hand, that several of the larger planets might prove more interesting. It is true that they are farther away from us, but we maintain that the bigger effort would be justified by the probably greater results. We have recently taken a special interest in the Constellation Pegasus or Equus, which lies, as we all know, between Andromeda and the head of Aquarius.'

The parents all nodded wisely to each other, trying to look as if they had known this all along. But what on earth – no, what in heaven's name – had all this to do with the Pony Club?

'British scientists have agreed that the atmosphere, the vegetation and the animal life (if any) on the stars of that Constellation may well resemble those which characterize our own world. Could there be human beings, or creatures, of similar intelligence, on Pegasus? We have no means of knowing, but our experts are doubtful. They question whether the soil there could produce anything but grass. Should this be true, only grazing animals could live there – cows, say, goats or sheep. I have assumed that this is true and I decided, therefore, against a manned flight. Our first rocket was designed to carry a single horse.'

The audience began to show a new interest. The speech was just beginning to make sense. A horse? Good show!

'But we had certain difficulties over money. In order to please some critics in Parliament, therefore, we replaced the horse (while we were still in the planning stage) by a *pony*. This could mean using a rather smaller rocket. That is the present plan, the rocket is under construction, and the time has come to choose a suitable Astrohorse. I need hardly tell you that the pony chosen will go down to history among the famous horses of the world. His will be a name to set beside those of Bucephalus, Black Bess, Marengo and Winston. He may well be associated with what men may yet call our Finest Hour.'

There was loud applause from the humans present and prolonged whinnying from the ponies.

'I cannot disguise from you the fact that I came here today with a double purpose. I looked forward, on the one hand, to an excellent day's sport – and that we have certainly had – but I also wanted to see whether we had here in Dorset a suitable pony to undertake this scientific mission – a pony that might be dedicated to a Higher Purpose. And I am glad to tell you that such a pony has been found. He is here this afternoon and I shall presently ask him to step forward. But what qualities, first of all, will the chosen Astrohorse need? He must be fit and not too big for the rocket we are constructing. He must be calm and brave. He must be ready to learn the technique of space exploration. He must be a fitting and creditable ambassador from the earth to whatever creatures there may be in Pegasus. He must have intelligence, a cool head and presence of mind.'

All the humans present began wondering which pony could have all these qualities. The ponies looked at each other in wild surmise.

'Today I perceived many of the necessary qualities in many of the ponies, but only one (I thought) possessed them all. As he and his rider were also the winners in one of the events, I will ask the Judges' permission to present that trophy first. We shall then be able to

applaud at the same time the winner of the Musical Gates Competition and the World's First Astrohorse. Will Prune come forward, with Miss Jennifer Starling.'

There was a moment of stunned amazement, followed by a storm of cheering mixed with an undercurrent of laughter which Sir Tracy did not notice. He gave Jennifer the silver trophy and patted Prune on the neck. Raising his hand for silence, he continued as follows:

'I should perhaps add that my valued colleague Dr Starling who, with Jennifer, is Prune's present owner, has already agreed to this pony's new career. He was first in Musical Gates and will now be first at the Gateway to the Universe. And I am sure that you all join with me in applauding Jennifer for making this sacrifice in the cause of Science.'

There was further loud applause and then Sir Tracy presented the other prizes, including the Junior Jumping Trophy, shared on this occasion between Mischief and Unbeatable. If there was a pony sorry for himself that day it was Prune. 'Gosh!' he said to himself, 'I've overdone it this time! However, I'll soon convince these scientists that they have backed the wrong horse.' At the moment, there was nothing he could do about it. He was led away to a horse trailer with 'ASTROHORSE' already painted on the side of it. He looked around to see whether there was a nosebag handy but the man in charge laughed and said, 'Sorry, nothing to eat. You'll be on a special diet from now on!' Close by, Spice was being led into another trailer, followed by Pat with a whole armful of apples. 'Just a nice ride to Southampton,' she was telling him, 'and then a short sea voyage to Guernsey. I'll meet you there on the quayside and we shall have a lovely time. Don't worry, little Spice!' '*Don't worry,*' echoed little Neville. 'You'll *soon* be there!' Prune snorted from the other horse trailer: '*Soon be there* indeed! What about *me*? I have to go a million miles on a slimming diet and nobody knows whether there is even a stable at the other end! And what's all this talk of Jennifer making a sacrifice to the cause of science? Who is making the sacrifice – the girl or the pony? Me or her? She or I? (Which is it?) Anyway, who's the victim? *I am.* And who gets the credit? *She does!* It's unfair! But why, *why* did I win at Musical Gates, letting Sir Tracy think me a genius? Foal that I was to make such a mistake. Look what I've let myself in for! My lucky stars, why was I ever called Prune in the first place?'

Over by the Judges' Tent, Jennifer was talking to Sir Tracy Evans; pointing out to him that she was now without a pony.

'I quite see that, my child,' said Sir Tracy, 'but your father tells me that you can have Skylark – that pony he is leading towards us, rather lame at present, I am told. It won't be the same – I realize that. No other pony can be quite like Prune; that, I'll admit, is undeniable.'

'But, but, but . . .' stuttered Jennifer.

'Believe me – I do understand . . .'

'But, actually, Prune was pretty usele – '

'Indeed, I can see that – very pretty indeed.'

'I'm not heart-broken, really I'm not . . .'

'Well, you are being very brave. But it is hard to lose an old friend, I know. You will be able to see him, mind you. We shall keep him fairly busy to be sure, but he will have a rest period every Sunday afternoon between 3 and 4 o'clock. You can call then, but don't bring him anything to eat. He will be on a diet.'

'I'll remember that. Now, Skylark – '

'He's not the same pony – quite, quite! But I'll do my best to make it up to you. With Skylark I'll give you a new saddle and harness, a new rug with your initials in gold, a new trailer with your name on it, a new hard hat and whip and a special instrument for taking stones out of horses' hooves. How will that do?'

'Oh, thank you very much,' said Jennifer earnestly. 'You are terribly generous. Honestly I don't deserve all that!'

'Oh, but you do! Some girls would have burst into tears at the thought of losing their best friend. But you took it very well – no doubt, for your father's sake.'

'For *Daddy's* sake?'

'Well, he designed the rocket after all. Now, one other thing. Since you have been so good about this, I'll give your new pony, Skylark, the *title* of Astrohorse. We'll make him Prune's Deputy or Stand-In, just in case Prune should be absent on any occasion. This will give him a salary or rather a retaining fee; enough to pay for his food, club subscriptions, and so forth.'

'Thanks,' said Jennifer, 'thanks a lot!'

In a corner of the collecting ring, Daisy was preparing to lead Smokey home to his stable. He was now the only pony she had left. Nobody wanted so old a pony and she herself would be gone in a few weeks' time. What was to be done? It was true that her father did not mind her leaving Smokey behind. He was welcome to his share of the grass in the paddock. But what sort of a life would he lead with no other pony to talk to? And what would they do with him in winter, there being nobody now to fetch him water, hay and straw. 'Poor Smokey!' she said as she led him homewards. 'What *am* I going to do with you?'

## 8

## SPICE GOES ON A VOYAGE

WHEN the trailer reached Southampton, Spice could see very little of the town or the docks. He could feel the jolting as the wheels bumped over a level crossing. He could hear a ship's siren and the cry of the gulls. He could smell the sea air and a mixture of other smells difficult to describe – fish being certainly one of them. The trailer stopped, went on, and stopped again. There was a period at rest, with more hooting and rumblings in the distance. A rough voice called out, 'Where shall we put this 'orse?' and another, more distant, shouted back, 'In Number Five Shed, Bill!' Instructions were given to the driver, the trailer bounced and swayed, back and forth, and then came to rest. Bang, crash! The doors were pulled open and Spice was led down a wooden ramp and presently tied to a ring-bolt. A man placed a bucket of water near him, and then Spice was left to himself. He began to look about him and form his first impression of Southampton.

Number Five Shed was the last in a row, open-sided like the rest and facing on the quayside. There were railway lines between the shed and the edge of the quay and, somewhere to the left, a great deal of activity which Spice could not understand. Then, from the right, gliding very slowly and towering above the quayside, came a great big ship, gleaming white and grey in the sunlight with several tugs fussing about her. Spice was afraid at first, pawing uneasily and wondering whether the ship was going to smash into the quayside. Nothing of the sort happened, however, and he watched the ship sidling nearer and nèarer until there was a faint bump as she touched the wharf. Ropes were tightened round bollards, gangways were run out, and a barrier dragged across the quayside to separate the passengers from the friends who had come to meet them. How important this was became quickly obvious. From the right came the sound of scurrying feet, pelting along the jetty. Number Five Shed faced on the quayside to which the big ship was tied up but its side, on Spice's left, lay along a smaller wharf which led back towards the Docks Entrance. Peering round the corner, which he was just able to do, Spice saw a much smaller ship tied alongside. He had hardly had time to take this in, however, before a crowd of teenage girls came running round the corner. More and more scurried along the small wharf, passed the point where Spice had been left, and sprinted past his shed towards the big ship's gangway. And as they caught sight of it they began to scream.

Poor Spice reared and plunged, scared out of his wits. What could the noise be about? Why the panic? Were all the warehouses on fire? Was the ship sinking? He whinnied at the top of his voice, hoping that someone would let him out before the building collapsed. But nobody took the least notice of him. All the girls swept past, with eyes only for the big ship, where a small group of young men had appeared on deck. They were oddly dressed and carried musical instruments. Calm again after the crowd had passed, Spice could see that their hair style was very similar to his own – a fringe falling forward between the ears. All the screaming was apparently directed against them, but whether hostile or friendly Spice could not imagine. While he was trying to make up his mind two men appeared from the back of the shed, one wheeling a trolley and the other carrying an armful of hay. The hay was for Spice and the man who had brought it paused for a moment to pat the pony's neck.

'What's all the noise about?' asked the man with the trolley.

'Don't you know?' said the other. 'It's the Death Watch Beetles, just back from Tangier!'

At that moment the young men began to play their guitars and sing. The girls were making so much noise that little of the music could be heard. Now and again, however, a few words came over. 'My girl's a honey. . . .' 'She's, oh, so sweet. . . .' 'Whenever we kiss. . . .' Then the screaming would grow louder and the rest of the verse would be lost. Scared as he had been at first, Spice presently found his hoof tapping the ground in time with the rhythm. It didn't make too much sense but the pony had to admit that the beat was exciting. The tune could have served, at a pinch, for a Musical Ride. It would not be as good as the Post Horn Gallop but there was something about it which a pony could appreciate. What were those words – something about a girl so nice, or the girl is mine? Tum-te-tum, tum-te-tum . . . and then all that yea, yea, yea stuff? Spice thought that if *he* had a little girl, one all to himself, he might compose a song of his own. Then he remembered that he *had* a girl – a child called Pat, who had promised to meet him at the other end of his voyage. His song could be about her. Then, if he could find three other ponies, and a guitar or two. . . . Yes, they could be the Horseflys . . . and – who knows? – Top, perhaps, of the Pops!

When the Death Watch Beetles had gone ashore and the crowd dispersed, Spice was led away from Number Five Shed, away from the big ship and round the corner. There lay the much smaller ship, her upper deck far below the level of the wharf. Spice looked down with alarm. Worse was to follow, however, for canvas bands were placed under him, a winch rattled, a derrick swung, and there was Spice, dangling in mid-air! He was deeply offended, but kicking did no good and he presently found himself sinking down, down, down into the hold. He glimpsed the words 'TORTOISE – GUERNSEY' on a lifebelt, then he was through a last hatchway and was glad to feel the deck beneath his hooves. A minute later and he was in a stall which had been rigged up in the hold. There was another stall beside it and Spice was cheered to think that he might expect company. Half an hour later, sure enough, another pony was lowered down the hatch. This creature's name was Dotty, and Spice soon began to suspect that he was weak in the head.

'My dear pony,' he babbled, 'I am going to the most wonderful job! You know Guernsey, I expect? Well, I have an appointment at the Castle. The owner of it – I forget his name – a Marquis I think, or is he a Duke? –

was wanting a pony for his grandchild. There were simply scores of ponies wanting the job but I was the one chosen. A question of looks, I imagine, and brains;

that, and knowing something of high society. I am to have a gold-plated manger – '

'A *what*?' asked Spice.

'A solid gold manger and a silver bucket, with another pony to act as companion. I don't like to be ridden, of course, by anyone less than Hon.'

'Does it feel very different – to be ridden, I mean, by a Hon.?'

'Indeed it does. Quite, quite different. Not the same thing at all!'

'And what about a princess?' asked Spice. 'Would that be different again?'

'To be sure it would! Princesses! I have known dozens of them. But this job at the Castle will be as good, really, as Buckingham Palace. Velvet, you know, instead of wood shavings. I expect there will be a band on the quayside when I go ashore.'

Dotty was still talking wildly about his brilliant future when the ship sailed. It was dark by then and there was a stiff breeze, the ship rolled and Spice felt far from well. All night the engine throbbed, the ship wallowed and the wind sang in the rigging. Spice could not sleep in any case, but Dotty's chatter would have been enough in itself to keep him awake. Half a dozen times Dotty began all over again, 'Did I tell you that I am going to the Castle? I expect there will be a guard of honour on the quayside. Not the nobleman himself, mind you, for he is a Royal Duke. He'll send someone else – a General, perhaps – to represent him. My loosebox will be panelled in walnut, with champagne served in a platinum bucket.' Ten minutes later he would begin again, 'Did I tell you . . .?' and Spice longed to say, 'Yes, you did, and I didn't believe a word of it!' But he restrained himself and made some pretence of being interested. As it grew light, Guernsey was sighted, and the little coaster was headed for St Peter Port. The rolling motion stopped as she rounded the pierhead, and a few minutes sufficed to tie her alongside the jetty. 'Oh, not *again*!' Spice groaned, but there was no way of avoiding it. He dangled once more in mid-air, but descended this time on the quayside. Soon afterwards Dotty stood beside him. No red carpet had been laid, and there was no reception committee to meet him. There was in fact no sign of anyone coming to meet either of them. Apart from a few men doing the work of unloading the *Tortoise*, the quay was deserted and so remained for nearly half an hour. Spice began to wonder whether Pat had forgotten all about him.

The *Tortoise* had come in ahead of her expected time but at 7.30, the hour when she was due, a shabby estate wagon appeared on the quayside with a trailer behind it. Out of the car stepped a grey-haired and terrifying figure in tweeds and breeches, followed by a couple of bored-looking teenagers. It was Miss Helliwell-Hackett, Proprietor and Chief Instructor of the Ponibrake Riding Academy. Striding over to Spice, she looked him over and growled, 'Not bad at the price – not bad at all. A good bargain if ever there was one! He'll be perfect, don't you think, for the Beginners Class?' This question was addressed to Joyce, the elder of her sleepy assistants. It was Olive, however, the other one, who replied, 'What about the other pony?' For the first time the formidable lady noticed the second pony, until then rather hidden by the first. '*That?*' she said. 'I know nothing about *that*. This one is mine, I'm sure.' Olive looked doubtful and the other girl now spoke up. 'Would you have got this one, Ma, for the price you were willing to pay?' There was something of an argument at this point and Spice thought, with a sinking heart, of the Riding Academy for which he appeared to be destined. As for Dotty, he was still expecting the Press photographers. 'Hard luck, Spice!' he said. 'Your girl must have changed her plans. They often do, you know. Don't know their minds from one minute to the next. So she asked the Riding School to take you on. Nothing more likely, I should say. In fact I should have been surprised if she hadn't. Well, well – better luck next time! Is that a Rolls-Royce coming this way?'

It was not a Rolls-Royce but a rather battered Morris Traveller. It drew up behind the trailer and out jumped – Pat! Spice let out a whinny and Pat ran straight towards him, followed more slowly by her mother and by young Neville. In a moment her arm was round his neck and an apple in front of his nose. 'Spice!' she cried, 'Spice *darling* – I'm so sorry we were late. Never mind, you'll soon be home!' At this point Miss Helliwell-Hackett turned to Pat's mother and said, rather stiffly, 'Is this your little girl's pony?' 'Oh, yes,' was the reply. 'We found him over at Melbury – he comes from Miss Dedleigh-Sirkett's Riding School.'

'So that this other one must be mine?'

'If you were expecting one, I suppose that will be the pony you have bought. What an odd-looking creature!'

'Odd!' cried Miss Helliwell-Hackett. 'He looks completely lunatic!' As for poor Dotty, he muttered to Spice that there was evidently some mistake, and that the Duke would sort it out in no time. 'Can you imagine *me* in a Riding School?' he asked indignantly and Spice admitted that he could not. In point of fact he could not imagine Dotty playing any useful role in any establishment. But he refrained from saying that, and the two ponies went their several ways; Dotty into the horse-trailer and Spice towards the town on his own four hooves.

It was a walk of several miles, with Pat leading and the car going ahead. Pat followed the road to the southward, trudged up a longish hill and then mounted when they were out of St Peter Port and away from the traffic. Spice eventually found himself trotting up a drive with fields and meadows around and an old house ahead. This was De Lacy Hall, where Pat lived with her mother and father. Pat made him circle the house and came finally into the stable yard behind it. Looking about him, Spice could see that this was a perfect place to live. There were two looseboxes and a harness-room. He could smell the hay in the loft overhead and glimpse the grass in the field beyond. There was a white-fenced paddock and a promising sort of orchard. And there, coming towards him, was the friendliest dog in the world. He was a Dalmatian in parts, although not the more obvious parts, and he was called Shandy. Spice and Shandy became great friends in a matter of minutes and it was the dog who now made the pony welcome and told him what a splendid home he had found. There were three children in all, the eldest, Nigel, being away at school but due back for the summer holidays. There was a flourishing Pony Club in the neighbourhood, with lots of Rallies and Gymkhanas at which the ponies and dogs could meet each other and gossip. As for Pat, she was terribly good over bones and apple peel, hay-nets and biscuits. There was a ginger cat, too, called Sherry. 'To catch the mice?' asked Spice. 'Well, I suppose that *was* the idea,' replied Shandy, doubtfully. 'But I don't think he does. The only time he saw one, he said, "Eeek!" and jumped into Nanny's arms.' Nanny, it appeared, was the special friend of both the dog and the cat.

It was early summer and Spice found that he was to spend each night in the paddock. Shandy came to see him just before the dog's bedtime, and asked whether he had everything a pony could want.

'Well,' said Spice, 'it would be nice to have another pony to talk to. Of course,' he added hastily, 'we shall always have lots to discuss, you and I. But, after sunset, when dogs have gone to their kennels – well, a paddock can seem a bit lonely.'

'But didn't you know?' said Shandy. 'Didn't Pat explain? There is another pony coming – a girl pony called Fairy. She should be here next week. That is what the second loosebox is for!'

Spice realized, after Shandy had said good-night, that De Lacy Hall was the ideal home and that Pat was the perfect girl. They would do great things together, and so in fact they did. But sometimes Spice would remember that day in Southampton and the dream he had dreamt of a pony quartet being Top of the Pops. He did more than dream now. He began to compose his first musical number, called, 'Me and My Girl'. Actually, the title had been used before, but he did not let that worry him. Gradually, the song began to take shape: and this is eventually how it went:

*Me and My Girl*

A honey (says Spice) and all things nice.
She's pretty and just turned nine.
A honey she is – you can say that twice –
But note that the girl is mine.

Everyone stops and everyone stares
When I come trotting to the Meet.
And some look jealous, but then – who cares?
*I* look so smart and *she* looks so sweet.

These latest songs, they start girls squealing,
It's not the music, just the beat.
Whenever we jump I get that feeling
Without her I'm not quite complete.

I've never known a girl so sprightly,
So well turned out, so clean and neat,
With reins so firmly held, but lightly,
She rides so well and looks so sweet!

# 9

# ASTROHORSE PRUNE

It is difficult to imagine why Sir Tracy Evans had ever thought it possible to make an Astrohorse out of Prune. It was perhaps the pony's name that took his fancy, just as it had attracted Jennifer's father, Dr Starling. But the Piebald Pony had few of the qualities which an Astrohorse should possess. Nor, for that matter, did he even want to engage in Space Travel. So the scientists at Newcombe Jettage found themselves landed with a difficult customer. A wild sort of animal at the best of times, Prune tried to show them that they had got the wrong pony. At the first rehearsal he refused to enter the Space Ship. When eventually coaxed into it, he refused to come out again. He was just as difficult as he could be and would, I think, have been sacked after the first week had it not been for the incident of the Stable Door. Prune had never forgotten an idea first suggested by Mischief (see page 17) and he now resolved to try it. Each day Sir Tracy Evans would look into his stable and say, 'Good morning, Prune! Getting on all right with your astral navigation?' Then he would walk off to see how the Space Ship was progressing.

'Stars,' said Prune, 'are what Sir Tracy likes best. I'll help him to see some new ones!' He waited, therefore, until the upper half of his stable door had been left unfastened and ajar. Then he stood near it, ready for action. All he needed was to hear Sir Tracy's footsteps and time his shove perfectly. The trap was set and the scientist was sure to walk into it.

Unfortunately for Prune, he had chosen the wrong day. Sir Donald Doddering, the President of the Royal Society, had arrived the night before, wanting to see what progress was being made. He and Sir Tracy were on the worst possible terms, and there was nothing friendly about their meeting. It was suspected, indeed, that Sir Donald would have liked to close the whole establishment and use all the available money to build himself an enormous telescope. 'We don't have to *go* to the stars,' he argued. 'All we need is to have a good look at them.' 'Oh, rubbish!' shouted Sir Tracy, and the argument had continued all the evening. Early next day – the day of Prune's ambush – Sir Donald was up in good time, resolved to see everything and find fault with everything. He decided to begin with the stables, muttering to himself that Sir Tracy would certainly have backed the wrong horse. There was no love lost between these two famous scientists but they did resemble each other in one respect. Their footsteps were alike. To Prune, therefore, it was obvious that Sir Tracy was approaching and at pretty much the usual time. In point of fact Sir Tracy was at his desk, writing a letter to the Prime Minister: a letter in which he said exactly what he thought of Sir Donald and his Telescope. So the President of the Royal Society was alone. Hearing his footfall, Prune put his head behind the stable door, chose exactly the right second and put all he had into a quick and powerful shove. 'Bang!' Sir Donald was on the floor in a sitting position, his left eye swollen and his head in a whirl.

About him the constellations and planets were revolving with a quite unusual speed and direction. He understood in an instant a whole series of astronomical problems that had puzzled him for years. He was light-headed and weightless for a moment and then fell back, completely stunned. Peering down in horror, Prune saw that he had knocked out the wrong man.

This, you would have thought, would have been the finish of Prune as an Astrohorse. Far from it – Sir Tracy was delighted! From this time he began to think Prune a genius – a pony of quite Exceptional Intelligence – a pony (he exclaimed) in a million. With Sir Donald in hospital, he could feel safe from interference. He pressed on with his work and refused to hear a word against Prune, for whom he now professed an unbounded affection. As for Prune, he became desperate, for his daily misbehaviour was no longer even reported to Sir Tracy. There seemed to be no way of escaping the voyage to Pegasus. But then he had another and better idea. He suddenly showed a new interest in his work. Instead of shying away from the Space Ship, he began to peer into its control room and study the equipment. Dr Starling, who felt rather responsible for Prune, was glad to notice this change in the pony's behaviour. He spent hours in explaining the use of the controls and Prune, nodding his head, seemed to be taking it all in. 'Now *this* lever,' he would say, 'sets off the booster rocket, which gives you additional speed. Push it round to figure B, and then back to neutral at A.' There was no harm, of course, in Prune's pushing the levers about, for the Space Ship was still on its side outside the Engineering Department. It would be erected, nose-upwards, at a later stage. In the meanwhile, all the experts were hard at work and Prune was as occupied as the rest. '*This* dial,' said Dr Starling, 'shows how much fuel has been used, and how much is left. . . .' Prune noticed that there was already a little fuel in the tank, probably as some form of test. He nodded his head again.

Some days later there was a conference of all the experts in Sir Tracy Evans' office. They sat at a long table and reported progress.

'Mechanically,' said Dr Starling, 'the ship is ready to fly. We only need to move her to the take-off position and you could blast off tomorrow.' 'That's splendid,' said Sir Tracy, 'but what about the scientific instruments she is to carry?' 'Not ready yet,' said Dr Focus. 'We have been having some difficulty with the sideview cameras.' So the conference went on, the scientists agreeing, incidentally, to send a copy of their report to Sir Donald Doddering, who was said to be convalescent. 'He will be glad to hear,' said Dr Focus, 'that our difficulties have now been mostly overcome.' 'Of course,' chuckled Sir Tracy, 'that will cheer him up a lot. I shall myself send him a wreath.' 'A *wreath*, Sir Tracy?' 'Some flowers, I mean, for his bedside.' Then Sir Tracy sniggered again and asked for news of the Astrohorse. 'He is doing very well, Sir Tracy,' said Dr Starling. 'He is keen to learn and has already mastered all the essential controls. His progress has been quite astonishing over these last weeks. Mark my words, that pony is going to make history. I wish he were here at this table, so that we could all congratulate him upon the wonderful progress he has made.'

While the scientists were all at the conference, Prune had wandered over to the Space Ship, as he had recently been doing each day. He checked his space helmet, as he had often done before. He took his seat in the control room and closed the outer door. He noticed that there was still some fuel in the tank and – yes – a booster rocket in position. Calmly and efficiently he went through the drill for take-off. He released the safety mechanism, switches 4 and 5. He put Dial E to 'Ready'. He threw the starting levers 7 and 8 and pushed the ignition button 9. He made the light signal on which the starting superviser would begin the count down. He did everything he had been taught and did it in the right sequence. The only thing wrong was that the Space Ship was lying on its side, resting on a frame outside the engineering shop. . . . Having done all the right things, Prune pressed button Z and sat back with his eyes shut. The men in the workshop were astonished to see the Space Ship surrounded by a cloud of smoke. They were amazed to hear a loud hissing and whirring. They threw themselves flat on the ground as the hiss became a scream. They covered their ears when the scream became a shriek. They finally said 'Gosh!' when they saw that the Space Ship was in rapid flight!

The Space Ship had been built on a frame which pointed, as it happened, towards the central building where Sir Tracy had his office. When fired off, the fuel in the tank was enough, with the booster rocket, to send the Space Ship whizzing at a height just above ground-level and very slowly gaining altitude. In a matter of seconds, however, the flight was over. The Space Ship crashed into the side of the central building at fourth-floor level.

'Yes,' Dr Starling was saying, 'I could wish that our Astrohorse were here in person!' A second later the wall collapsed behind him with a crash of falling brick and splintered glass. And through a cloud of smoke and dust there appeared the Perspex nose of the Space Ship, through which again the scientist could glimpse the face of the Astrohorse. He was there, as Dr Starling had wished, in person. . . . With a final 'whooosh!' of the booster rocket, the Space Ship lurched forward and fell – smash! – right across the conference table. Sir Tracy Evans found himself looking the Astrohorse in the eye, separated only by the Perspex. To Dr Starling he now yelled, 'Take this creature out of my sight!' It was at this instant that the floor fell in. . . . Over the rest of this dreadful scene it is best to draw a veil. The scene was, after all, too confused to describe. It would be wrong, however, to omit all reference to the arrival of the telegram. After lying, stunned, for some minutes, Sir Tracy lifted a typewriter off his chest and scraped some of the pastepot out of his hair. He rose unsteadily to his feet, wondering whether it was all a nightmare and whether he would presently find that he had fallen asleep at his desk. It was at this moment that Dr Focus appeared, climbing over the ruins and holding an opened telegram. 'From Sir Donald,' he explained breathlessly, 'a telegram of congratulations.'

Next day there was another conference, held now on

NOTES

the third floor. The scientists met in a room of which the sides were shored up with timber, the windows blocked with sheets of hardboard. Sir Tracy had a bandage round his head, Dr Starling had crutches and Dr Focus had his arm in a sling. Few of the others had escaped injury, and two were absent in hospital. Their meeting was short, however, and they had only the one duty to perform. Within a very few minutes they had agreed to dismiss Astrohorse Prune and appoint his deputy, Skylark, to the vacant post. Dr Starling was asked to inform Skylark (and Jennifer) of the new appointment. As for Prune, the word was 'Out!' In theory he should have left with his tail between his legs and his head hanging downwards with shame. He was, in fact, delighted. He had never wished to be an Astrohorse and he now thought himself pretty clever to have gained his freedom. More than that, he was immediately offered a good job as a circus clown. The story of his flight in the Space Ship was reported in the newspapers, and a circus proprietor realized that an ex-Astrohorse with a sense of humour would be an attraction to the public. And an attraction he certainly proved. For years afterwards crowds would come to see his Act. He was shot off twice nightly in a miniature space ship, which flew across the Big Top and crashed into a canvas building which was put there for the purpose. He would bow to the crowd afterwards and scamper off to the performers' tent. The complaint about Prune had always been that he was a bit of a clown. He never, in fact, learnt to be sensible. He discovered instead that he could gain applause by being still *more* of a clown. He is very happy these days and is never sorry that he chose the life of the Open Road. Even Sir Donald Doddering has forgiven him and came once to the Circus. He was offered a front seat but refused it with understandable caution. 'I would prefer,' he said, 'a seat well at the *back*.'

## 10

# SPICE ON PARADE

SOME months after Spice came to live at De Lacy Hall, Pat went on a short visit to London. Her mother's purpose in going was to visit Pat's grandfather but Pat had a different idea. While glad to see her grandfather, what she really wanted was to see the Life Guards. Each day, she had been told, the guard is changed at a place called the Horse Guards. This she was determined to see, and so she did. The day was fine and the spectacle was all she hoped it would be. Across the Horse Guards Parade came the men in scarlet and polished steel, their swords glinting in the sunlight, their black horses stepping proudly and their plumes nodding above their helmets. Through the archway they clattered and into a courtyard where as many troopers again were drawn up in line. The sentries were relieved and the old guard rode off towards Buckingham Palace. Pat had been sent postcards of London but the real thing gave her a tremendous thrill. 'Only one thing could have made it better,' she told her mother. 'And that would have been to have Spice there.' Her mother was a bit doubtful about this. 'Don't you think he would look rather small, alongside those big horses?' Pat agreed that there was a certain contrast in height but saw how the difficulty could be overcome. 'What we should have is a Children's Troop, all on ponies!' Her mother promised to write to the Prime Minister about it, but her letter (if actually posted) failed to produce any immediate results. Pat remembered her plan, however, and often referred to it, pointing out what the Queen was missing.

The Queen's representative in Guernsey is the Lieutenant-Governor, usually an Admiral or General. A General held the position at this time and Pat's father told the children one day that His Excellency was to visit their house 'for drinks', as he said. 'Can I pass round the nuts?' asked Neville eagerly, but Pat was against it. 'He eats them all himself!' she explained and Nanny agreed that this theory was at least partly true. 'No,' said Pat's mother finally, 'no passing round the nuts. But you can stand at the end of the avenue and watch the Governor arrive.' Some discussion followed as to whether Neville was to wear his sword, and as to which of their neighbours' children should be invited. 'I'll fire a salute from my cannon,' said Neville (who had visited the Tower of London), adding 'Boom! Boom!' to illustrate the effect he had in mind. 'You'll do no such thing,' said Nanny firmly. 'The idea!' Pat's father was on Nanny's side so far as guns were concerned but regretted, all the same, that there could be so little colour on these occasions.

'Last year,' he went on, 'I visited Halifax, Nova Scotia, where they have a splendid fort on a hill. A postcard I saw there showed the gate, with a mounted sentry on either side. I asked about this and was told that the local children had formed a sort of cavalry unit. They have their riding lessons at a place just under the fort and they appear in full uniform on state occasions.'

'Like the Life Guards?' asked Pat eagerly.

'Well, not exactly. They actually call themselves "The Junior Bengal Lancers"!'

'But why *Bengal*, when they live in *Nova Scotia*?' asked Pat's mother.

'Don't ask me. Perhaps Geography is their weak subject. But they look terribly smart, with their turbans and lances, and Halifax couldn't do without them.'

Pondering this over, Pat asked herself whether she and her friends could not do something on the same lines. Why shouldn't they form their own troop of Life Guards? Better still, why shouldn't they provide the Governor with a Cavalry Escort? When this brilliant idea occurred to her, Pat nearly ran indoors to tell her mother. Then she thought again. Wouldn't it be more fun to make it a surprise? She knew that her parents were to be away for ten days, returning not long before the Governor's visit. The rehearsals could be held then but Nanny would have to be told. She was let into the secret that afternoon and promised to tell nobody. On her advice, Pat decided to limit her army to a total of eight; herself as the officer, Neville as the trumpeter and six troopers to form the escort, three abreast before and after the Governor's car. Some frantic telephoning led to a first meeting in the harness-room, the six others being invited to become soldiers for the occasion. All were glad to serve and there was an argument on the question of costume, Carola wanting to manufacture uniforms and helmets. But that idea was finally rejected as impracticable, all agreeing to wear black coats and hard hats. The rehearsals began on the very day that Pat's father and mother left for Paris. Nanny wheeled the old pram, to represent the Governor's car, and the drill was worked out in detail. At the third attempt the ponies began to see what was wanted, and Spice looked very proud of his position at the head of the column.

When the children were gathered in the stable yard, planning the date for the next and final rehearsal, the old gardener, Mr Le Gallienne, came to refill his watering can at the stable tap. 'What are you up to?' he asked Pat. 'And what is that pram supposed to be?' So he had to be told that it was going to be a surprise and was all deadly secret. He swore to tell no one and agreed that the Governor would be terribly impressed.

'It puts me in mind,' he said, 'of the old days with the Guernsey Militia. I was a Corporal then. No, we had no cavalry that I can remember. There were horses, though, for the artillery; and of course the officers were mounted. We would put on a big parade on the Belvedere Field, with crowds of people to watch. Yes, they were great days.'

'Did they fight any battles?' asked Neville.

'No, not that I heard of. The people who came nearer to fighting battles were the Germans, who occupied this very house and were all ready to fight in case the British landed. Look, they made loopholes in the wall over there, and had barbed wire between those posts. They were ready to fight, sure enough, but they were never attacked. They surrendered later on but I didn't see that, being a prisoner.'

The children decided after this, with Mr Le Gallienne's approval, that their escort should represent the

Guernsey Militia, protecting the Governor in case the Germans should come back again. Mr Le Gallienne promised to lend them an old trumpet which would do for Neville to hold; and if he could get no sound out of it, that might be just as well.

On the day of the Governor's visit everyone at De Lacy Hall was busy. There was the parking problem, to begin with, which meant keeping all traffic off the front drive when the Governor was due to arrive. There were problems, too, about sherry glasses and ash trays, filter-tipped cigarettes and soda-water siphons. Pat and Neville were told to wash and put on their clean clothes, but their absence from that point was scarcely noticed, and Nanny told Pat's mother that the situation was in hand. So it was, with eight riders approaching the front gate by an indirect and concealed route. Old Le Gallienne opened the gate from the lower meadow and, just before the Governor was due but after all the other guests had parked, the Guernsey Light Cavalry took up their posts at the gate. Pat on Spice was on the right, Neville with his trumpet was on the left. Nanny was hidden nearby with a camera. Two minutes later the Governor's car appeared, with its flag on the bonnet. Lady Bleasdale sat with her husband in the back seat, Captain Fitzgerald (the A.D.C.) sat beside the chauffeur. The car drew to a halt as Pat rode forward, saluting with her whip. 'What on earth . . .?' began the A.D.C., but Pat gave the word of command and the escort moved into position, three riders in front with Pat, three behind with Neville in rear of them. The chauffeur then drove slowly on amidst the clip-clop, clip-clop of the ponies.

Leading the parade was Spice, the proudest pony in the world.

Imagine the surprise felt by Pat's father and mother

when they caught sight of the approaching cavalcade! 'Look!' said the guests to each other as they crowded round the drawing-room windows. Smartly turned out, with harness polished, the young riders trotted up to the front door and then formed in line facing the front of the house. His Excellency and Lady Bleasdale were helped out of the car and made welcome by the host and hostess. As they moved indoors, Pat saluted again with her whip and the Governor gravely raised his hat in return. Their duty done, the escort went round to the stable yard, where the children dismounted. And there they were found by Captain Fitzgerald, who had been sent to look for them.

'Well done, Pat!' he called out. 'May I have a word with your troops?' The children gathered round him, still holding their ponies, and listened. 'His Excellency has asked me to congratulate you on the smart appearance and drill of his escort. He realizes how much trouble you must have taken, and wants to thank you for it. Well done, all of you!' The children all said that they had loved doing it.

'Now there's one other thing,' the A.D.C. continued. 'You may not have heard the story, but the avenue up to De Lacy Hall was the scene, some time ago, of a very daring crime. Some sheepstealers, in league with the De Lacy herdsman, killed off and stole a whole flock of sheep in the meadow here. They were desperate men, well armed, and might have killed anyone who tried to stop them.'

'When was this, sir?' asked Carola, who was the most romantic of the children.

'In about 1605 or thereabouts. Now, Hugh de Lacy came home from St Peter Port while the crime was being committed. His daughter was his only companion and he had no sword. All he could do was to watch and listen. There was little to *see* on that night but one sound he recognized – his herdsman's voice! He knew that the servant he trusted was a friend of the sheepstealers.'

'Couldn't he have raised the Clameur de Haro?' asked Carola.

'Only if he had known how to say the Lord's Prayer in French.'

'And he didn't?' asked Pat.

'Evidently not. Do you?'

'Well, no, actually . . .'

'So you can't blame him, can you? However, he did his best. When morning came, his herdsman came to report the loss of the sheep. "Ah," said Hugh, "you must come and give your evidence at the Royal Court." And as soon as he had the wicked herdsman in court, surrounded by the officers of the law, he cried out, "Seize that man!" So the herdsman was thrown into prison.'

'Serve him jolly well right!' said Pat.

'Quite so,' said Captain Fitzgerald. 'Now His Excellency knows about this crime and has concluded that this is a dangerous part of the country, where some further incident might happen at any moment. He feels, therefore, that he and Lady Bleasdale would be safer if they had an escort when they leave. Will your troop of cavalry be available in an hour's time?'

'YES SIR!' said the children in chorus. So the Governor left under the same escort, parting with them at the gate. The evening was drawing on by that time and the woods, in the failing light, had a touch of menace. Carola looked around with a shiver and said, 'I say, do you think the Governor was *really* worried about bad men? I mean, have there been any crimes here *recently*?' Pat laughed and said, 'Never heard of any! I'll tell you what I *have* heard, though – that there might be some cheesestraws going in the kitchen!' The troops cantered back to the stables in no formation at all, just as if the bad men had been after them.

That evening Spice told Fairy that this had been the most wonderful day of his life – not realizing, perhaps, that Pat was saying the same thing to her mother.

'Yes,' said Spice, 'I led the parade! And I wish all my old friends had been there to see. . . . Some of them used to say that I was too small to do anything important. Oh, they should have been there! Nice ponies they were. There were eight of us, with Unbeatable and Mischief, the competition jumpers, Brighty almost as good and Skylark a wonderful pony in the show ring. Dunblane and Prune were pretty useless, I'll admit, although quite pleasant in their way. But I wonder sometimes what has happened to them all. There was Old Smokey, for example. I hope he has found a good home – old as he is. And Skylark – there was a pony for you! I should have thought he would be famous by now, an animal with all that talent. No one would have guessed, perhaps, that I should do as well as I have. But Skylark, now, there is a pony that should have gone right to the top!' Had Spice been studying the newspapers, instead of chatting with Fairy, he would have known that Skylark was already on the path to fame. He was indeed on his way to joining that select band 'Horses of the World'. Of the eight ponies he is the one to have made history, the one whose name no horse will ever forget.

## II

# SPACE-AGE PONY

WHEN Prune was replaced by Skylark, the saddest person in the world was Jennifer. She had hoped desperately that Prune would prove more useful in Space than he had ever been on the ground. But the inevitable happened and her darling pony Skylark was destined to become the world's first Astrohorse. Left without a pony (for she wanted no other) Jennifer could only watch and wait. With the Space Ship repaired after its first disaster, with the great work nearing completion and her father's career at stake, Jennifer could not stand in the way of Skylark's career, and Skylark she now saw very seldom. He was spending long hours in his space-suit, learning the system of manual control and studying the science of astro-navigation. He was, as Jennifer realized, an exceptional pony, but how much rather would she have kept him in her own paddock, available for the next Gymkhana and a hot favourite in 'Musical Blocks'. As for Skylark, he tried to tell her that he would do just one space voyage and then retire. This would have been small consolation for Jennifer even if she had been able to understand. She hated the idea of space travel. What if he never came back?

Jennifer was so worried about this that she asked her father one evening about the space pony's chances.

'Well,' he said, 'I feel pretty certain that my rocket

will get there. I think that it should land safely; and Skylark is a sensible pony, mind you. We certainly picked a winner in *him*. But I won't deny that there are risks. And the main risk, as I see it, concerns the return flight. Should the rocket be damaged in landing, our pony might find it impossible to take off again. He could stay there, mind you, with plenty of grass, but with no way, perhaps, of return.'

Jennifer cried herself to sleep that night, thinking of her dear darling Skylark, all by himself on a distant star. She knew, however, that she must be brave when the day came for the flight called 'Operation Pegasus'. And brave she was, saying good-bye to the Astrohorse without a tear. 'See you again soon!' she said, smiling, and no one knew of her inward worry. There was a whole crowd of people there – professors and experts, reporters and cameramen. Richard Dimbleby gave a running commentary for the B B C and Jennifer was near enough to hear his words even when she dared not look. 'It is a beautiful day here at Newcombe Jettage and the great space rocket towers above me, gleaming silver in the sunshine. Princess Margaret is wearing a becoming frock in sky-blue and Lord Snowdon, I see, has brought his camera. The lift is slowly ascending to the platform from which the pony will enter the Space Ship. I can just glimpse his helmet as he goes on board. The suspense is almost unbearable. The time is now 10.29 with just twenty seconds to go. . . . Ah, the count down has begun!' Another voice could be heard saying, 'Seven, six, five, four, three, two, one. . . . Contact!' Looking up now, Jennifer saw a white cloud billowing round the

Space Ship. She heard people saying 'Oh!' and 'Oooh!' and 'There she goes!' She saw the great rocket mount into the sky with ever-increasing speed. Then she heard a voice over the amplifier saying, 'Pegasus I, Pegasus I, inform base now of any defect in your equipment. Do you notice any failures in the control system?' A clearly transmitted 'Neigh!' was the response, relieving Jennifer's immediate anxiety. So far her darling pony was safe. But the terrible question still remained unanswered, 'Would Skylark ever come back?'

Aboard the Space Ship, hours later, Skylark was at the controls, reporting a successful flight with a fine view of Aquarius (where, he thought, it was raining). Things were going so well that he had time to read the last issue of *Horse and Hound*; turning from that to the *Instructors' Handbook*, published by the British Horse Society for the Pony Club. There was a spelling mistake on page 7 – 'Manege' should surely be 'Manage'? – and Skylark resolved to inform the Committee. He ate the tablets which he carried – apple, carrots and oats in a concentrated form – and told base about everything he could see. Hours later again, after Jennifer was in bed, he reported that the nearest star in the Pegasus Constellation (Pegasus A) was now in sight, the Space Ship on course and all going well. At breakfast next day Jennifer heard that the Space Ship was approaching Pegasus (A) and might be expected to land in an hour's time. After a further and final period of suspense came the radio announcement that the Space Ship had evidently landed but that all contact had been lost. The announcer explained the official view that the ship's radio had been damaged by the shock of impact. There was no reason to suppose that the Space Ship had crashed or that Skylark would be unable to return. After that there was no more news for days, for weeks, and even for months. Jennifer's father told her not to give up hope but most people thought that the flight must have ended in disaster.

In fact, however, the rocket had landed more or less safely. The shock of landing *had* destroyed the radio but Skylark was able to open the hatch and reach the surface of Pegasus (A). He realized then that the Space Ship would never fly again. Some of its most vital machinery was smashed beyond repair. Where he stood beside the wreckage he could see all about him the rolling grass-covered hills of Pegasus. He took a mouthful of grass – it was excellent! He could glimpse in the distance the glitter of running water, and there, within a few yards, was a hoofprint! Pegasus must be inhabited. Going over to examine the hoofprint, however, Skylark noticed something very odd indeed. There was that one hoofprint and beside it, a second; but no other marks in sight! He began to picture a two-legged horse able to jump a mile, but further guessing proved needless. There was a flying object coming over the hills – it was coming straight towards him – moving like a bird but big as a horse – it *was* a horse – a horse WITH WINGS! A few minutes later the winged horse stood beside him!

'You poor, poor animal!' said the winged horse to Skylark. 'How sad to have lost your wings. . . . How I sympathize with any horse who has to travel in a thing like that!' The winged horse snorted towards the Space Ship and looked pityingly on Skylark as on a creature compelled to use crutches. Skylark had to explain that no horse on Earth has wings, that he had come from Earth and meant (if he could) to return there. Skylark's new friend was called Dizzy and it was from him that the Astrohorse learnt how the winged horses had come to live where they did. 'The first winged horse was Pegasus himself, after whom the Constellation is named. A man called Bellerophon mounted Pegasus and attempted a space trip to Zeus. But he forgot to fasten his seat strap! There was some turbulence when Pegasus was stung by a wasp.'

'So he fell off?' asked Skylark.

'He made an emergency landing. But Pegasus continued the flight on schedule. There was fog round Zeus at the time so that he was re-routed to this Constellation, where his family have lived ever since.'

'And are you all born with wings and able to fly?'

'Oh, dear, no. We go to a flying college, study for months and pass examinations, only getting our wings when we complete the course.'

Skylark enjoyed meeting Dizzy's friends but felt terribly handicapped, being able to do no more than walk, trot, canter and gallop. As for jumping, he did not even mention the word! He wanted to return to Earth and to the Pony Club. Above all, he missed Jennifer. So he asked Dizzy whether he might go to the Flying College.

'My dear Horse!' cried Dizzy. 'The very thing I was going to suggest.'

It was all arranged and Skylark found himself attending classes in the Theory of Flight and Advanced Space

Navigation. So much had to be learnt that the College was called Cramwell. Months later he passed his first examination and went on to practical work under the Chief Instructor, a Wing Connemara. He was fifth in order of merit at the Passing Out Parade and felt very proud of the wings he was now qualified to wear. After a day or two of celebration he decided that the time had come for his second space flight; this time, back to Earth. He said good-bye to his college friends, shook hooves with Dizzy, and took off on the long journey home. Round his neck he carried a nosebag and a bucket of water. Both were discarded before the flight finished and the bucket is now in orbit round the moon, being often mistaken for a satellite. His navigation was very good and his flight ended in a perfect four-hoof landing between Market-Snodborough and Piddlethwaite; not six miles from his point of departure. Once he knew where he was, he could fly back home in a few minutes. Looking from her window, Jennifer suddenly saw a Flying Horse in the paddock! Wings apart, it looked just like her own darling Skylark . . . same colour . . . same mane and tail. . . . Good gracious, it *was* Skylark!

By the time Jennifer reached the paddock and put her arms round the pony's neck, a crowd had begun to collect. Within an hour or two the cameramen and reporters were lining the hedge and asking for a statement. But Jennifer led Skylark back to his stable and posted up a notice to say that the Astrohorse was resting. After all, he had had a pretty big day! But there was no dodging the publicity after that. On the Saturday he was taken to Buckingham Palace where he had an audience with

the Queen, being made a Horse of the British Empire (H.B.E.). He appeared on the Tonight show, being interviewed by Cliff Michelmore himself. And next day his

Speech to the Nation so disorganized the BBC that Perry Mason lost his case that evening, his client receiving a life sentence before anyone could intervene. Many politicians were furious at the picture which appeared of Skylark being given sugar by Mark Bonham-Carter. 'And the P.M.,' they raged, 'didn't even know that the Astrohorse is a Liberal!' Even *The Times* gave half a column to the event and the *New Statesman* was alone in seeing the whole thing as a plot devised at the Cavalry Club. There could be no dispute about it. Skylark was the most famous horse in the world, and assured of his place in the Olympic Team. *One* gold medal for Britain seemed now virtually certain.

But Skylark was the last pony in the world to allow his life to be spoilt by success. He allowed Kellogg's to name their new breakfast food after him, but he refused to appear on the stage or on the films. He made it clear that all he wanted was a quiet life, pottering round his own paddock and stable and flying each winter to the West Indies. The Minister of Civil Aviation issued him with a Pilot's Certificate and installed a control tower in the corner of the paddock. He was made an Honorary Air Commodore and a Colonel in the Kentucky Militia, a Doctor of Science of the University of Sussex and (many years afterwards) a Fellow of All Souls. He declined all other honours, including a Life Peerage, and preferred to live simply with his friend Jennifer and his neighbours of the Pony Club. As for Jennifer, she was the happiest girl in England. 'Aren't you lucky?' her friends exclaimed, 'to have the only Winged Horse in the World!' But Jennifer merely smiled and said nothing. She did not really care whether he had wings or not. It saved the fares, admittedly, when travelling to Jamaica, and she avoided all that tedious business of flights cancelled or delayed. But her great joy was simply in having him back again, safe and sound. She had gone through misery when his space flight began, worse misery when she believed that it must have failed. Then had come the great moment of his return, followed by the relief of knowing that his days for space travel were over. They have lived together ever since and Jennifer now has another pony for show-jumping. 'It is not that he is actually *disqualified*,' she is careful to explain. (There is nothing in the *Manual of Horsemanship* to say that Winged Horses are ruled out.) 'But I don't think the others would think it fair – do you?' And we must all agree, surely, that she was right. She came in third at the last Gymkhana – that is, in the Jumping Event (Under 11) – but everyone knew that she had another and better pony at home, and that is, actually, where Skylark feels happiest, rolling in his own meadow and talking to his own friends. He is the most modest of ponies, never talking of his adventures or boasting of what he can do. After that one lecture to the Royal Society on 'Ancient Myths in the Light of Modern Research' he has been seen very little in scientific circles. Only rarely, indeed, does he unfold his wings.

Each autumn, however, when the wind begins to grow chill, when the fallen leaves are being collected for the bonfire and the birds start chattering about the travel literature they have read, a certain activity is seen in Skylark's paddock. The neighbours notice that the winged horse has strolled over to the control tower. 'He is calling for a Met. Forecast,' they tell each other. 'I hear it is to be Bermuda this year.' Then Jennifer comes out of the house in her very warmest clothes, suitcase in hand. She mounts and holds on to the neck strap, leaving the reins loosely knotted. She places the headphones over Skylark's ears and can presently hear that cockpit chatter all pilots seem to love: 'Control tower calling, control tower calling. That you, Skylark?' ('Who *else* could it be?' Jennifer wonders.) 'Runway clear for take-off. Wind East-South-East, Force Three, Visibility . . . etc., etc.' Skylark begins to stretch his wings, testing each pinion to see that it is in working order. Then he walks over to the leeward side of the paddock, facing downwind until he receives the final 'O.K.' from ground control. Then he turns into the wind, trots, breaks into a canter and finally gallops. At full speed, with wings now beating furiously, he takes a big jump. He is airborne! Away he sails, he and Jennifer disappearing westward and rising through dense cloud into brightest sunshine. They will return, with the birds, when the winter is over. But back at Newcombe Jettage the scientists are at work on a new scheme, this time for exploring the Milky Way. No pony is to be chosen on this occasion, however. This time they talk of sending a cat.

## 12

# SMOKEY GOES HOME

ALL alone at Dedford Ditchbury, Smokey was the last of the ponies and wanted, apparently, by nobody. With winter coming on, Daisy's old father decided to advertise again, asking only a small price but insisting that the pony should have a good home. 'I can't look after him,' he explained. 'Not in winter, I mean – what with my rheumatism and all.' He received only one offer, however, and that by post from the other side of Wiltshire. This letter came from an old man called Pedro Neroni, who said that he was in the entertainment business and needed a pony for his show. Remembering Christmas Pantomimes, in which Cinderella's coach is often drawn by ponies, Daisy's father agreed to sell. After Mr Neroni had gone, however, taking the pony with him, the old man learnt that Neroni was merely a Punch and Judy Showman, who used a small cart to take his theatre and puppets from one fair ground to another. It was rumoured, moreover, that his last horse had died of starvation and ill-treatment. 'Poor old Smokey!' said the neighbours. 'He won't last for long, dragging that cart all over the countryside.' It was too late, however, and the sale had been in order, with the money paid and the pony led away with apparent kindness.

It was in fact a miserable life to which Smokey was condemned. The cart was quite heavy and yet had no room, it would seem, for oats or bran. Neroni would drive up the steepest hills, never setting foot on the ground or giving any help. And all the time he would be talking to his puppet 'Punch'; never to his pony, nor indeed to anyone else. When he drank too much beer, which happened after each show he gave, he would talk more loudly and Punch would sometimes answer back. One day he told Punch that their next stand would be at Bridport Fair. 'We'll do well there,' he said, 'if this weather holds and if this lazy pony will get us there in time.' 'Whip him,' said Punch, 'that will make him trot.' 'I will so!' said the showman, and poor Smokey knew that another long march was ahead of him. Worn out, sore and hungry, he eventually reached Bridport on the eve of the Fair. Roundabouts and shooting stalls were being set up on the fairground and tent pegs were being banged in under flaring lights. Pedro Neroni found a corner of the field for his theatre, tethering Smokey in a spot where all the grass had already been trampled into mud. He himself slept in some lodging on the other side of the town, returning early next day for business. 'We always do well,' he told Punch, 'at Bridport, and look, the day is going to be fine!'

From mid-morning onwards the Punch and Judy show attracted small groups of children. Some were scornful, saying that television was more worth watching. Others stood entranced, sucking their thumbs, but had no money to pay for a stool. Late in the morning two rather different children appeared, livelier than the rest, who took little notice of the show but showed great interest in the pony. The boy was called Martin, aged eight,

and he was attempting to control a sister called Bridget, who was barely four. They were known in their village as 'M and B'. 'Isn't he lovely!' said Bridget. 'And doesn't he look hungry?' said Martin. They ran to fetch grass from the other side of the fence and spent some time holding it up to Smokey who accepted it gratefully. They were still doing this when their mother came over to fetch them. As she approached, Smokey suddenly raised his head and looked towards her. A minute later she stopped and stared, then went up to the pony and said, 'SOOT! No, you were called SMOKEY in the end. . . .My old friend! Dear old Smokey!'

'You *know* him, Mummy?' asked Martin.

'He was my very own pony when I was your age!'

'Gosh! He must be very old now!' said Martin (boys have no tact).

'But he's a *darling*!' cried Bridget.

'And we have a spare stable . . .' muttered the boy, as if to himself.

The children's mother was none other than the Lorna of years before, the little girl who had since grown up and had children of her own. She would never have parted with Smokey had she known that he would end by pulling a wretched cart. She knew now that she must have him back. He would be a splendid beginner's pony for Bridget, with Martin to help look after him, and later, well, he could spend his old age at leisure. She waited until the Punch and Judy show ended, then walked over to Pedro Neroni.

'I see you have an old pony there. Could I persuade you to part with him?' But the cunning showman had been watching the scene when the two old friends had recognized each other. He saw his chance to make money.

'Sell my pony, Ma'am? No, I can't do that. He's too valuable to me, and of course I'm fond of him. How can I get round from one Fair to another without a pony to drag the cart? It's my living, you see. No, I won't sell old Smokey, not if you were to offer me a hundred pounds!'

'But he's too old to drag that cart!'

'Well, maybe he is, and maybe I have to use the whip to make him go. But I can't help that. It's the way I live.'

'But you don't feed him properly! Look how thin he is!'

'I can't afford to feed him much. This business is not as paying as it used to be. It's all I can do to feed myself.'

The showman turned to Punch as soon as Smokey's friend had gone, and chuckled to think how clever he had been. 'She wants her pony back, eh? Well, Punch, the worse he is fed and the worse he is treated, the more she will pay! Do you know what I shall do, Punch?' Punch evidently had no idea. 'I'll go on to Dorchester, like I planned, and then to Port Bygone and a few other places. And when I get back here again, that pony will look much worse. I'll see to that! She has a soft heart, that lady. I shall end by selling her the pony at the price of a Racehorse. That's business, that is. And I'll buy another horse at half the price! It's not everyone,' he pointed out, 'who would have thought of that!'

Lorna Lawkinson, now Mrs Strickland, may have had a soft heart but she was not at all stupid. She had guessed what Pedro Neroni was planning and she had no intention of allowing his plan to succeed. She came back that afternoon without the children but accompanied by a policeman. Coming up to Neroni she pointed to him and said, 'I must ask you to arrest that man on a charge of cruelty to animals. This is his pony, and you can see that the poor animal is nearly dead of starvation.' She walked over to Smokey, leaving the policeman to talk with Neroni.

'Is that your pony?' asked the policeman sternly.

'Yes – and what about it?' said the showman defiantly.

'Then you'll have to go before the magistrate on a charge of cruelty.'

'You can't prove anything! I'll bet the magistrate lets me off and tells you to mind your own business, and not meddle with other people's horses!'

'He may,' said the policeman. 'And then again he mayn't. But they are strict around here about cruelty to animals. A man the other day was sent to prison for three months, just for ill-treating a cart-horse. And Mr Strickland didn't give him the option of a fine. Three months it was – yes, and with hard labour!'

'Mr Strickland, did you say?'

'That lady's husband.'

'And he's the magistrate?'

'Chairman of the Bench, and about the strictest we ever had!'

'Strewth! I'm done for!'

'Looks like it to me. But I dare say the lady could drop the charge if she knew that you had brought the pony here for sale.'

Pedro Neroni raged and used the most terrible language. But he had to admit defeat. He agreed to sell Smokey for a nominal sum and was seen next day dragging his cart by hand towards Dorchester. There was no other horse for sale in Bridport nor would anyone have sold him a horse even if one had been available. 'I'm ruined!' he told Punch as he trudged away. 'I have no money for another horse. I'll have to give up this life and work like other people.' It may have been a jolt of the cart, but Punch seemed at that moment to nod his head in agreement. Mr Neroni now works as a fishmonger's assistant but puts on his Punch and Judy show at children's parties.

As for Smokey, he is now just as happy as he used to be when Lorna first rode him at Borough Farm. Bridget rides him each day but she is a nervous child and never wants to do more than trot. He is well fed these days and remarkably fit, considering his age. Martin rides another pony, quite young, who shares the paddock with Smokey. This gives Smokey what he needs, a listener; and one, incidentally, to whom his oldest ancedotes are new. Bridget will have to have another pony if she is ever to ride in a Gymkhana, but that won't be likely just yet. Nor, when it happens, will the Stricklands dream of parting with Smokey. He will be seen in their meadow for many years to come. And sometimes he will talk to the other pony about the time he was at the Dundreary Riding School. 'There were eight of us,' he begins, 'as fine ponies as ever you saw. Skylark, the Astrohorse, was destined to be the most famous, but all of us did well and even Prune, the silliest of them, has a good job, they say, in a Circus. Little Spice was on television the other day, the leading pony in a Guard of Honour, and Dunblane appeared in a programme called "This is your life", featured, you know, as the children's friend. But I was older than the rest, no show jumper like Unbeatable or Mischief, no champion at Musical Gates like Brighty. The others thought I was too old, even then, and guessed that I would never have a good home again. And I thought at one time that they could prove right. Yes, I have known what it is to be overworked and underfed. But even when things were at their worst, I knew that, somehow, some day, I should have a home like this. So I always say, to young ponies like you, "Never despair!" and they all nod their heads wisely in agreement. Actually, they don't know what hardship means, and so I tell them. And what do they reply?' He turns to the other pony for an answer, but none is forthcoming. Fond of him as the other pony is, he ceased to listen some time ago. By now that other pony is asleep.

*Some other Puffins you might enjoy*

## BREAK FOR FREEDOM

Ewan Clarkson

Syla was a mink, and so dark brown she looked almost black.

The cage where she lived was identical with all the others, except for one thing – there was a loose staple in the floor of her sleeping box. And that was the way that Syla escaped from the fur farm to find a new life, free in a remote valley on the edge of Dartmoor, free to hunt and fish and play, and also to face the dangers of traps or sudden chills or fierce animals.

Ewan Clarkson is an expert naturalist and makes a fascinating story of Syla's year on the moor, her brief courtship with another escaped mink and her life with her cubs. At the same time he tells us about all the other inhabitants of Dartmoor, the birds and insects, snakes and rodents, till the moor seems as busy and complicated as the greatest human city.

For readers of eleven upwards.

## HORSE IN THE HOUSE

William Corbin

Melanie Webb was one of those girls who can't live without a horse, and the one she had was a winner, a white palomino stallion called Orbit. He was never out of her thoughts, and he waited all day for the moment she came home from school to ride him.

Then Mom and Pop went off to San Francisco, giving Melanie a chance to put her cherished plan into action – her secret wish to bring Orbit inside the house. One night Melanie went out to the barn to say goodnight to Orbit, but he was gone and the unoccupied stable was intolerably desolate and empty. Melanie felt useless, like a captain without a ship. Yet somewhere Orbit existed, and somewhere, she was sure, locked in her head was some little memory, a shred of a clue to the thief.